Angela Webber is well-known as a comedy writer and performer. Famous for her role as Lillian Pascoe on 2JJJ, she also co-wrote *Brunswick Heads Revisited* and *Regrets I've had a Few* and is a regular writer for television and radio comedy.

Richard Glover's crazed account of life in the nineties appears weekly in the *Sydney Morning Herald* and Melbourne's *Sunday Age*. He is also heard on radio in his role as Mr Magazines and makes fleeting visits to television.

Angela and Richard together wrote *The P-Plate Parent*, and Richard has also published *Grin and Bear It* and *Laughing Stock*.

THE JOY OF BLOKES

A survivor's guide to the men in your life

How to meet them
How to love them
How to eat their cooking

ANGELA WEBBER AND RICHARD GLOVER

ALLEN & UNWIN

ACKNOWLEDGMENTS

Thanks to Debra Oswald, Stuart Matchett, Margaret Miller, James Bennett, Kate McClymont and Paul Leadon.

© Angela Webber and Richard Glover, 1994

This book is copyright under the Berne Convention. All rights reserved. No reproduction without permission.

First published 1994
Allen & Unwin Pty Ltd
9 Atchison Street, St Leonards, NSW 2065 Australia

National Library of Australia
Cataloguing-in-Publication entry:

Webber, Angela.
   The joy of blokes.

   ISBN 1 86373 752 9.

   1.Men - Australia- Humor. I Glover, Richard. II Title.

305.310994

Designed and typeset by Modern Times Pty Ltd
Printed by Australian Print Group

10 9 8 7 6 5 4 3 2 1

CONTENTS

Introduction vii

Chapter One 1
BLOKELAND
or Four Encounters with the Modern Male

Chapter Two 19
MAN CRAZY
Surviving the Dating Game

Chapter Three 31
ARGUING FOR BEGINNERS
or The Six Sorts of Sorry

Chapter Four 45
STUNT HOUSEWORK
and the Trial of Somebody

Chapter Five 55
SEX
The Eternal Triangle (You, Him and Sharon Stone)

Chapter Six 67
FATHERHOOD
The New Man in Action

• THE JOY OF BLOKES •

Chapter Seven 79
MID-LIFE MAN
or A Sudden Interest in Aphids

Chapter Eight 89
SHOPPING FOR CLOTHES
or The Quick Way to End a Marriage

Chapter Nine 99
THE DECLINE OF MAN
Blokes at Their Worst

Chapter Ten 109
SUDDENLY SINGLE
or Meeting Mr Possibly Right

Chapter Eleven 119
MAN THE MENU
Select from Our Extensive List

Chapter Twelve 129
THE BATTLE OF THE SEXES
A Final Word

Index 140

INTRODUCTION

Why do blokes walk around the house naked? Why do they play Air Guitar? Why do they keep little jam jars full of coins in their bedrooms? And what exactly is Stunt Housework?

Australian males have always been a mystery. It's not only the tender words they use to greet their closest buddies — 'g'day you clueless loser' — it's also the peculiar thrill they get from going under the house with a torch. Or from packing a crowded boot. Or from prising off a tight gherkin jar lid in front of their bemused girlfriends.

It is true we live in challenging times — times in which it's hard to tell whether gender roles are changing rapidly, or whether, beneath the surface, everything's staying much the same. Or to put it another way: when Australian women finally smash through the glass ceiling, who's turn do you reckon it'll be to clean up the mess?

In the pages to come, we'll examine man from dating to divorce, from new age to old age, from housework to hunkdom. We'll study the peculiar nature of male self-esteem, discover how to rope blokes into housework, and document the world's worst come-on lines.

We'll also meet Blind Freddie, walk bravely into the danger zones of the modern argument, and detail that new mating call of the midnineties woman — the Female Fwooar.

Which brings us to another question: if women are really running with the wolves, does that necessarily mean men have gone to the dogs?

But before all that, it's time to meet the men of Australia, and spend a little quality time with them — calmly observing their behaviour in its natural environment. And we're about to meet four of them — the modern show-off chef, the home renovator, the traditional rev head and the new age BBQ-er.

Could your bloke be among them? Come with us now, up on your tippy-toes, as we quietly open the door, and peek into the hidden but exciting world that is Blokeland.

CHAPTER ONE

BLOKELAND

or Four Encounters
with the Modern Male

"In the tribes of the New Guinea highlands, men prove their masculinity by slaughtering a wild boar. In the deltas of Java, men scarify their chests with sharp rocks. And in Australia they try putting together Ikea furniture."

Encounter Number One

BLOKES AND COOKING

The Recipe for Disaster

Tonight he's cooking, but before he begins everything *must* be perfect. The knife on the cutting board, placed just so. The garlic in its own bowl ready for peeling. The benches sparkling.

'I mean, no creative chef can be expected to produce his best work in a *pigsty* like this,' he says. And frankly he's surprised you manage to achieve anything at all, those other six nights a week. But then *his* standards are higher. Much higher.

It's the most difficult show-off dish he can find in the recipe book. And in his hands it's a recipe for disaster.

The dish is Stewed Pork with Porcini Mushrooms and Juniper. And he's absurdly confident. Right up until the moment when he can't find the slotted spoon. And that's when his mood changes, and the emotional roller-coaster ride begins.

'*Someone's* moved the spoon,' he wails. 'Oh God! These drawers are a disgrace. How's a man supposed to cook? And who keeps moving things in here? It all changes every day. Can't we have some sort of *system* in here?'

He upends the drawer, and dedicates the next hour to repacking the kitchen. It's thirsty work. He'll just grab a low-alcohol beer while he slices the mushrooms. And that's when he lets loose an anguished cry. The porcini mushrooms — he's left them at the checkout. Oh God! It's too much, what with the missing spoon and now *this*. He hurls off his apron and stomps out to the garden with another beer.

Gently you must coax him back to his task. After all, the guests will be here in an hour. You suggest he uses normal mushrooms. *He* suggests you butt out. *He* knows what he's doing. He'll just use the normal mushrooms.

But now he's starting to get rattled. 'Who blunted the knife?' 'Who lost the vegetable peeler?' 'Why aren't the frypans in the frypan cupboard?' 'Why can I never find the grater?'

Suddenly it's Question Time and he's the Leader of the Opposition. And the Parliamentary language is not good. He's starting to bang the pots and pans around, and slam shut the cupboard doors — occasionally on his own thumb. His cooking may not be exotic, but his language certainly is.

As you shepherd your frightened children into the garden you can hear him making explicit threats to the cheese grater, and questioning the parentage of the electric mixer. Yes, the pressure's starting to show. He accidentally sends the punnet of juniper berries flying, scattering them across the floor, and whacks his forehead hard on the range hood. Maybe a splash of wine would help him calm down?

The recipe begins to swim before his eyes. 'Add the cubed pineapple.' What cubed pineapple? Whoops. Wrong recipe. You hear him muttering as he flips desperately through the book. 'What criminal moved it off the bloody pork page?'

And so it goes. Step after emotionally wrenching step. It's not just your dinner on the line, it's his reputation as a chef. Not that he's worried: under the influence of a well-earned Scotch his confidence is beginning to return.

This meal is going to be bloody fantastic. One of his best ever. The guests won't believe their taste buds. And the timing's perfect. Twenty minutes before the folks arrive and all he's got to do is the last step of the recipe.

He turns the cookbook page, and checks out that last bit of the recipe. 'Soak haricot beans overnight, then bake with pork for three hours.' He stares at the page in mute disbelief. How did this happen? Who can he blame? He gropes wildly into his befuddled mind. What would Keith Floyd do in an emergency like this?

Keep Drinking!

Of course. Keep drinking. And then whack the lot in the microwave, hoping for the bloody best.

Meanwhile the guests are arriving. Frankly, they are surprised to see your children in the front yard on such a cold night. But you usher everyone in, and offer a pre-dinner drink.

Now you're the over-confident one. Out in the kitchen only the dregs of the bottle are left, and your partner is red-faced and sweating. It's lucky the guests have brought their own grog.

While you fix the drinks, your partner swans in to greet the new arrivals, a fixed smile on his face. 'Just blanching the beans for the salad — dinner won't be long,' he says, 'it's going to be great.' You try to distract the guests. You talk about politics. You talk about the Olympics. You play a couple of rounds of Pictionary. You go out and get a video.

At 10.15 dinner arrives. And miraculously, it's a pretty good effort. Then it starts. The pathetic fishing for compliments.

'Bugger,' he says, 'I think the carrots could have done with a few more minutes.'

'Oh, no,' chorus the guests, 'they're perfect.'

'But, you've got to admit, I overdid the sesame seeds — jeez I'm *sooo* sorry.'

'Oh, no,' chorus the guests, 'they're perfect'.

'Well I guess they're not *too* bad,' he finally concedes — 'but the meat's really ruined.'

'Oh, no,' chorus the guests, 'it's perfect.'

The guests are not actually being insincere. At this time of night, they're so drunk and hungry that even the tablecloth would have tasted good. And so, around 2 am, having exhausted their stock of superlatives, they finally make their farewells — with your partner stumbling after them as they hurry to their cars. 'Just tell me one last thing — you don't think the zabaglione was just a little too sweet?'

'Oh, no,' they chorus out their windows as they accelerate down the drive. 'It was perfect.'

Meanwhile, you're back in the kitchen. Or what's left of it. It's a disaster. There's not a pot or implement that hasn't been used. Somehow he's managed to use pans you didn't even know you owned. As you start scrubbing, he wanders back inside. The drink's worn off and he's gone into a total decline, racked by self-doubt.

If only he hadn't put that extra spoonful of sugar in the zabaglione. He could kick himself.

'Oh no,' you chorus, 'it was perfect.'

'Yeah,' he says, with a wan smile. 'Maybe you're right. It *was* perfect. I think I deserve a drink.'

'And the best thing of all, darling,' he adds, snuggling up to you, 'is that whenever I cook, it's great knowing you've had a lovely chance to relax.'

• BLOKELAND •

Encounter Number Two

DO-IT-YOURSELF BLOKES

In the tribes of the New Guinea highlands, men prove their masculinity by slaughtering a wild boar. In the deltas of Java, men scarify their chests with sharp rocks. And in Australia they try putting together Ikea furniture.

Australian blokes will often offer to fix things. Don't let them. They'd be better off outside, trying to slaughter a wild boar, while *you* ring a plumber. Not that he'll let you make the call: what you think of as 'booking a tradesman', your guy regards as verbal castration.

Furious and defensive, he'll insist that he's going to do the job. His blokehood is in question. He's wound up, a wild bull pawing the dirt. He strides to the shed, determined to prove himself, and twenty minutes later emerges in his combat fatigues. Nail pouch hanging from his side like a gunslinger's holster, the hammer swinging wide. Blundstone boots and footy socks. Stubbies. Paint-splattered Expo 88 T-shirt. And his treasured tough-guy peaked cap, advertising Smithfield Truck Parts.

Thirty minutes ago he was a worn-out middle-manager, calmly reading the Saturday paper. Now there's so much testosterone coursing through his veins he can no longer speak English — he's talking Hardware, an ancient dialect of G-clamps and O-rings, of clouts and concrete, of paint strippers and masonry bits.

And it's then you hear the chilling phrase: 'No worries, Deb, I can fix this myself.'

It is a phrase that has been heard by generations of Australian women, and one that's often heralded quite startling results. For some women, a burnt-out kitchen. For others, a flooded basement. For still others, an unexpected move to emergency accommodation. But for the majority, what follows is just a lot of bad language and finally a late night call to the emergency plumber.

However, we're getting ahead of ourselves. *That's* still hours away.

As of yet, your bloke still hasn't broken the thread on the tap, smashed the plastic S-bend, or accidentally swung his pick through the water main. Forty-five minutes later, and already you've gone from a dripping tap to death in Venice.

Plus it's all your fault.

You watch as his panicked mind desperately gropes for a way to blame you for the tragic events which are unfolding under the sink.

Finally he has it. 'You went into my shed. You must have taken something. My big adjustable spanner. And that's why I had to use the small one. And that's why the whole thing's gone wrong.'

But still he's optimistic. And there's absolutely no need to ring a plumber. He'll just ring his mate Phil. *He's* got better tools. And *his* wife never goes into *his* shed and steals stuff.

Your fella wades into the hallway and makes the call. Phil comes over with his socket set, a wet suit and plenty of misplaced confidence. But, uh-oh, the crucial bit of his socket set is missing. Presumably it's been stolen by Phil's wife, Jenny. It's an epidemic of female crime and these guys are the innocent victims.

Mind you, it's not all the fault of the womenfolk. At least some of the blame, they've got to admit, belongs elsewhere — to the bodgy plumber who installed these pipes in 1952.

The boys set to work — repairing that damn plumber's mistakes with the few 'hopelessly inadequate' tools they have left. Now two masculine psyches are being put to the test.

And that's when the shocking language starts — expletive after angry expletive. They don't need a sign saying 'men at work'; the

• BLOKELAND •

> ## CELEBRATING HIS BLOKEHOOD
>
> *Eight things your bloke does when he needs to convince himself that he's a real man.*
>
> 1. Going under the house with a torch
> 2. Using an electric drill
> 3. Talking to the car repair man
> 4. Ordering hardware
> 5. Packing the boot of the car
> 6. Fiddling about with BBQ starters
> 7. Esky duties
> 8. Showing off with a snazzy corkscrew

whole street can hear how upset they are. And all because they don't seem to have a G-clamp.

They'll have to go to the hardware store. Phase two.

The Hardware Store

The hardware store is basically a very big bloke's shed. Staffed with people designed to make *your* bloke feel inadequate. Blokes in leather aprons. Blokes who've lost a finger. And blokes who can smell an idiot halfway across Plumbing Supplies.

They've seen it all. The blokes who've got raw sewage coming out their garden sprinkler. The blokes whose belt-sanders have run amok and harvested the shag pile. The blokes trying to act calm as they ask — 'and quickly please' — to buy something to put out a small electrical fire.

That's when they point your bloke towards the home handyman's friend — the F-Wit Range of fillers, screens, cover-alls and concealants. Product slogan: 'Stuff it in whenever you've stuffed it up.'

Of course, no real man would ever buy this junk. A real man might buy a single tube of woodfiller to conceal the nails in his cabinet making; your husband's built most of the sunroom out of the stuff. Three sheets of radiata pine, ten truckloads of woodfiller — which leaves the house with two problems. One is the lingering odour; two is the way the room shrinks in hot weather.

But the pressure's on now as the two men scan the F-Wit Range trying to spot a glue-based product which can fill a 30 cm hole out of which water is gushing at 80 km an hour. (The F-Wit Range has become a success story on the basis of making wild promises to cretins.)

And there it is, right in the middle of the shelf. F-Wit's Flood Buster — a $9.95 tube of filler which 'in most applications' will part the Red Sea.

Your bloke looks anxiously at his watch. In three minutes, the hardware store is closing. In ten minutes the State Emergency Squad will have to be called.

He buys the Flood Buster. Even though, in his heart of hearts, he knows this is final proof of what a dickhead he really is.

Not that he's going to admit that to you. Or to his pal Phil.

'This will do the trick, mate,' he says.

And — surprise, surprise — it doesn't.

Finally, at 11.30 pm, he and Phil admit defeat. And get *you* to ring the plumber.

And *that's* the worst moment of the whole day. When the plumber, woken from deep sleep, stoically rows in, shakes his head, and in front of you all puts that deceptively simple question to your husband:

'Mate, why didn't you turn off the main?'

Encounter Number Three

BLOKES AND CARS

Who can explain it? Inside the house, he's a slob. He throws his wet towel on the varnished dresser, puts his work boots on the couch and looks blank when you show him the Windex.

But outside, fussing over his vehicle, he's become a prissy perfectionist, hysterical over the merest smudge on his otherwise perfect duco. And would you mind if he borrowed your toothbrush to clean out the yucky edges of the odometer?

Clearly, this isn't just a car; it's a love interest. And as with any hot affair, he can't help lavishing presents on her. One week it's a fresh deodoriser, the next a set of lambswool seat covers. Then, to mark their first anniversary, a set of mag wheels.

And he's only really happy when they are alone, just the two of them, cruising in fifth, burning rubber and laughing with abandon like some crazy, carefree P-plater. Later, after the climactic wheelie, he lights a cigarette and flatters her about her performance, particularly her cute big end. After which they go parking together.

Many blokes have their first meaningful relationship with a car. And let's face it, she's a hard act to follow. *She* didn't talk back, *she* didn't demand equal rights, and *she* accepts her place is in the garage. For men, it must be very reassuring in these changing times.

Women think that you are what you eat; men *know* you are what you drive. Inside their cars blokes are still warriors, pointing their jousting stick up the road. To them, it's a deadly machine, breathing fire, roaring thunder to the world. What a shame that, to you, it's just a clapped-out Valiant with piss-weak steering.

On the other side of the tinted windscreen, the world is full of vague slights against his manhood, even if non-blokes can never quite work out what they were. What *you* noticed was a man cutting into the traffic. What your bloke saw was a provocative bastard out to prove he had the bigger penis. No way is he going to ignore the slight. Even if the other bloke *has* got a six-cylinder sedan.

And so the flags are down. The tape measures are out. Your bloke screams off at the lights, and starts to overtake the white Commodore, leaning out as he passes to give the finger and shout 'Eat my dust, loser wimp.'

It's then you hear the siren. That loser wimp is actually Highway Patroller Detective Neville ('Slugger') Stallone. And he's two arrests short of the free gold watch and the Wonderland family pass.

This isn't going to be pretty.

Watching your bloke grovel is not a good look, particularly once he gets down on his hands and knees and starts licking the dust from Slugger Stallone's boots. What a shame he's now lost so many points on his licence that you'll have to take over the wheel. It's the ultimate humiliation. Bring driven around by a girl. *And* while he's sober.

Not that he won't give you free advice on your driving. Constantly. You've held a licence for fifteen years, but suddenly you're back in driving school. You're heavy on *his* clutch, you're grinding *his* gearbox, you're taking the corners much too fast. Thank heavens, when ever anybody cuts in on you, he's happy to help out with the rude hand gestures.

But, licence or not, your man can still spend his Sundays in the garage, working up a sweat in the reverse missionary position. It's the way God intended. Bloke underneath, car on top: auto-eroticism at its most fulfilling.

BLOKES AND CARS: THE TEN COMMANDMENTS

1. Only blokes can drive properly

2. Only blokes can load a boot

3. The bloke in the other lane is a dickhead

4. Only a bloke can reverse park

5. Only a bloke knows the shortest route

6. It's the wife's fault the spare is flat

7. Blokes with red cars have larger penises

8. An orange light indicates a bloke must accelerate

9. Following a breakdown, it's a bloke's birthright to open the bonnet and stare inside as if he had a clue what it all means

10. Only girls drive Hyundais

• THE JOY OF BLOKES •

Encounter Number Four

THE BBQ BLOKE

It's a ritual that goes back to the dawn of time ... a man, a fire and a pile of burnt steak. Just like yesteryear, men are still hunters, searching for their prey in the dark, cold, uncharted landscape that is the back of your meat tray.

'There was blood everywhere,' they stammer as they emerge triumphant with a couple of cling-wrapped T-bones. And it's then the tribal ritual really starts — an ancient and sombre ceremony which has been passed down from meat-eating father to meat-eating son.

Once around a barbecue, the male of the species begins a long march backwards through the millennia of evolution. In your eyes he's on the patio, burning a couple of Big W breakfast thins, but in his mind he's back on the tundra, scorching a musk ox which he's just wrestled to the ground.

You see his mates Gordon and Darryl from the indoor cricket team standing around the kettle barbie, sinking stubbies, arguing about the best brand of BBQ sauce. But he sees his fellow warriors, lap-lapped and bare-chested, chanting the ancient hunting songs of their ancestors.

But, uh-oh, there's trouble amongst the tribesmen.

According to Darryl, your bloke's done it all wrong. Any nong knows you should start off with all the heat beads in one pile — not two. And he's left it too late to light the fire-starter. The whole thing's a bloody fiasco.

Gordon says that Darryl couldn't recognise a fire-starter even if it was down his shorts and well alight. And according to Gordon, they're both stupid since gas barbies are the go.

So they start arguing about how to light the thing, and end up fighting over who gets to use the tongs and who decides when to turn the meat. No wonder the food's incinerating.

But that's the way it's got to be. At a traditional Australian barbie, the host will always ask you how you like your meat cooked, and there are three options: burnt, bloody burnt or totally incinerated.

The Aussie Bloke's BBQ cookbook is a very slim volume. In fact there are only two recipes:

1.
THE OLDE STYLE AUSSIE BARBIE

You will need 2 kilos of rump steak, a slab, snags for the kiddies and a coleslaw whipped up by the missus.

Ingredients: Steak and snags.

Preparation time: Depends on sobriety of the host.

Cooking instructions: Commence inferno in BBQ with 10 packs of fire-starters; add steak; incinerate till fire brigade arrives. Assist brigade to douse down flaming paling fence. Allow fire chief to retrieve steak which is now 'perfect'. Serve on bed of tomato sauce. Guzzle slab to remove taste.

Or you could try the more modern and multicultural barbecue, as perfected by Australia's thousands of yuppie blokes:

2.
THE NEW STYLE AUSSIE BARBIE

Ingredients: 2 kilos of meat comprising spatchcock, marinated prawns, quail, turkey and sage sausages and a coleslaw whipped up by one's significant other.

Preparation time: Unclear. Depends on the extent of Brian's tizz about the spatchcock's stuffing. And his sobriety.

Cooking instructions: Commence inferno in BBQ with 10 packs of fire-starters. Add spatchcock, marinated prawns, quail, turkey and sage sausages. Incinerate till fire brigade arrives. Assist brigade to douse down flaming pergola. Allow fire chief to retrieve spatchcock which is now 'perfect'. Serve on a bed of wild rice. Guzzle Beaujolais to remove taste.

But no Aussie BBQ could survive without a secret marinade — and one which only *your* bloke knows about. Luckily *The Joy of Blokes* is able to publish one for the first time ever — breaking a bloke code going back generations.

So here it is:

• BLOKELAND •

> ### Grandpa Webber's Never Before Disclosed Secret BBQ Sauce For Steak and Chops
>
> Mix equal quantities of tomato sauce, Worcestershire sauce, sweet vermouth and brown sugar. Add a clove of garlic, chopped not crushed. (Sweet sherry can be substituted for the vermouth, if you have it.) Brush on the sauce each time the meat is turned. Fantastic!

N.B. According to family legend, Grandpa Webber received this recipe from a man who had stowed away on Count Von Luckner's yacht *Seeadler* in the late 1930s. Count Von Luckner was a famous U-Boat commander and legendary German BBQer.

N.N.B. All blokes' special BBQ marinades or sauces come complete with an extremely unlikely Boy's Own story like this one, often involving war exploits.

N.N.B. Contrary to what you may expect, the authors did not invent either this story or the marinade (which incidentally is very good). Both are reproduced precisely as handed down by Grandpa Webber.

Not only is Pa's Marinade a beaut, it's also guaranteed, just like any culinary adventure, to keep your bloke busy for hours — leaving us free to continue our journey into the world of men.
And, hang on tight, we're about to hit the first speed hump ... it's Chapter Two, dating.

CHAPTER TWO

MAN CRAZY

Surviving the Dating Game

"You stumble out of the restaurant, both desperately wondering how to stop the evening having a premature ending. After all, there'll be plenty of time for that later."

You've met him. You like him. But how do you get through to the typical Aussie bloke and tell him you're interested? As a modern woman, you could always tell him what you feel. But that's not what all the advice manuals suggest. That would be far too simple.

They say women must indicate they are sexually attracted to a man by sending him some subtle messages through body language. According to these books, you should:

> 1. Lean forward, with your eyes wide and staring.
> 2. Thrust out your chest.
> 3. Moisten your lips and allow your tongue to dart along your lower lip.
> 4. Be extravagantly expressive with your body.

And men will instantly know that a woman acting in this way is either a) sending strong sexual messages of lust and romance, or b) is having a fit.

These are the delicate moments when it's all expectation and desire. And, providing he's not mistaken your messages and rung an ambulance, it can be a time of delight. The accidental touching of knees. The girlish laughter at his jokes. The frantic effort to keep interested in his rather lengthy life story.

And at the end of it all it's natural to kiss him. After all, it may be the only way to stop him talking about himself. But before you get carried away with that kiss, you should know that, on average, 250 types of bacteria are exchanged in a single mouth-to-mouth encounter.

This isn't passion, it's a science experiment. You might be hours off mating, but your bacteria are already breeding. What tarts! It's hard to believe, but *they're* not even waiting for the coffee.

You stumble out of the restaurant, both desperately wondering how to stop the evening having a premature ending. After all, there'll be plenty of time for that later.

Right now it's time for you to start communicating in the age-old language of lovers: The language of euphemism. Ask him, 'I wonder if you'd like a cup of coffee at my place?' and watch, delighted, as he goes wild at the idea. 'How did you guess?' he'll say, 'I'd kill for a coffee. I just love the stuff. Coffee — I'm addicted to it.'

In fact, he hasn't drunk coffee in fifteen years. It brings him out in hives. But he'd say anything for a ticket back to your place.

Doing It

You're back in the flat, sitting on your couch, and the three inches between your bodies seems like an uncrossable divide. It's a deep chasm that only the brave would dare to leap; the chasm of feared rejection.

By kissing him, you figure that you've already put enough on the line — in particular, your health. It's up to him to make the next move. But *his* anxiety is worse: after all, if he's not quick he might have to drink the coffee.

He starts leaning toward you, shifting his weight onto his left buttock, and twisting his spine as he imperceptibly works his arm along the back of the couch. You, meanwhile, are carefully inching

DATING DISASTERS

Certain tell-tale signs which reveal that the person you are dating may turn out to be a no-go:

1. As an ice-breaker, he shows you his rash
2. He tries to recruit you to Amway
3. He cautions against your dessert choice as: 'A little fattening for you, I think'
4. He takes you to a lingerie restaurant
5. He pays for a drinks with a hot credit card
6. He arrives with his wife
7. He offers you a pamphlet on Tantric Sex
8. He corrects your pronunciation
9. He alerts you to the dangers of horizontal stripes
10. He argues the toss about whether you slept together in 1987

your knees towards him, aware of every centimetre; aware of every wrinkle and fold in the couch cover, as your thighs continue their glacially slow march. The tension is unbearable.

Fifty minutes later, your body is tingling with extraordinary sensations. That's right — it's cramp. The two of you have been sitting too long without moving. And you're now both frozen rigid in poses that'd take an Indian yogi a lifetime to perfect. What a shame your heartthrob's back has just gone into spasm, and you've lost all sensation in your lower limbs.

This is safe sex at its very best. There's no way you can possibly do it now.

Sex with an Invalid

Experts talk about extended foreplay, but the six weeks that your new bloke has spent in traction does seem a *little* excessive. Still, those hospital visits have given you time to really get to know him. You know he likes grapes, you know he thinks his physio is a sadist, and you known he's now really worried that Jack and Jennifer won't get back together again in *Days Of Our Lives*.

Better still, you're beginning to get back a bit of feeling above the knees.

Then comes the night he's discharged, and he limps into your flat — an explosive bundle of rampant hormones and performance anxiety. And all while you are facing a challenge of your own: how to have uninhibited, wild and passionate sex while ensuring he doesn't glimpse that patch of cellulite.

You orchestrate a darkened room, and lie thrilling as you feel him slide into bed beside you. Gently, you snake your hand across towards him, and feel something hard beneath the sheets. Don't panic. It's just his crutches. The rehabilitation period has begun.

Living Outside the Law

One day you may wake up and realise you haven't been home for three weeks. You've bought a second toothbrush and your clothes are evenly divided between your house and his. That's when you start toying with the idea that you should live together. Think again. You could instead consider buying a second set of clothes.

After all, it's one thing to share with him the most precious moments that life can offer. And quite another to share a bathroom.

Anyway, which bathroom should you share? Do you move into his flat and make a brave attempt to housebreak his best friend Mikey — a man who prepares breakfast by boiling cocktail frankfurts in an electric jug? Or do you invite your new fella to move in with you and risk reducing your flat to the state of his? Whichever you choose, on the freeway to love there's a price to be paid, and you're about to hit the toll-booth full bore.

As it happens, your new bloke decides he likes the idea of shifting into your place; perhaps because, unlike his, it hasn't been condemned. And so he moves in. Just you and him. And his exercise machines, his surfboard, his electric piano, his amps, his box of athletic supports, his 'Good Campers' certificate from Scouts ... and his Great Dane 'Sargey-Boy'. All into your one-bedroom, bijou apartment.

The good news is that you're going to spend a lot of time in bed together. It's the only place you'll fit.

But of course it's all worth it. Suddenly you've got someone to come home to at night, someone to share a joke with over the breakfast table, and someone to assure you that the bathroom scales must be broken. To him, your body shape is just fantastic and for that opinion you're willing to put up with a lot. Which is just as well.

Only a week ago you saw your bloke shimmering through the rose-coloured glasses of early romance. Now you can barely make him out through the brown scunge on the shower-screen door. It never went that funny colour before *he* moved in.

That's the thing about most men — however endearing they may be, when they walk into your life they always seem to leave a fine layer of topsoil.

Relax. Sure, he's dropped bundles of clothes in every room of your flat, and left newspapers all over the lounge, but this is just a man's way of marking out his territory. And it's hardly fair to blame him for not offering to vacuum the floor — after all, he hasn't seen one in years. In the flat he shared with his mate Mikey, you couldn't get near the floor for the motorbike parts and the dirty laundry.

Back then, he and Mikey didn't think clothes needed to be washed. They thought they just needed to be *rested*. They seemed to think their undies had got all hot and sweaty, and all they needed to do is calm down, take it easy, maybe just slob around lying on the floor for a week or two, and — fantastic! — they'd be ready for another outing.

Since then you've encouraged him to wash; you've introduced him to the washing machine, or as he knew it, The Big White Shaky Machine Inside the Room With Tiles.

But your new bloke still has a serious disability. He suffers from selective blindness. He can't see dirt in the kitchen, has serious trouble locating the washing-up, and is totally unable to make out the shape of an ironing board — even using the map and identikit photo that you've thoughtfully provided.

Strange, he doesn't have this sort of trouble finding that last can of beer in the fridge. Nor his condom packet — which he can locate even in the dark with one arm tied behind his back and blindfolded. Not that we want to go into all the details of your intimate moments here.

Blind Freddie

The truth is, like 98.6 per cent of Australian women, you've shacked up with Blind Freddie. And you'll recognise Blind Freddie as soon as you see him. He's the man standing in front of the five metre long bread display in the local supermarket, shouting out to his partner, 'Darling, where do you think they hide the bread?' And he's the bloke wearing the dark glasses swivelled up onto his head, demanding:

'Where the hell have you put my sunglasses?'

But despite it all, living together brings its own delights — the mornings spent admiring his body in a pair of cut-off jeans and a torn T-shirt, the lazy weekends snuggled up together.

And naturally, you'll spend most of your time luxuriating in bed. It's heaven: you and him, and — oh, yes — Sargey-Boy, who's on total bed rest since that distemper scare.

Yes, these are the days to cherish — days spent running your hands through his hair, sharing a leisurely meal, having him jump with abandon into a hot bubble bath with you. And it'll be even more fun when your bloke comes home, and takes Sargey-Boy for a bloody walk.

Meeting the Outlaws
— A Hostage Situation

Parents' attitudes to living together vary considerably. The mother of the woman in a de facto marriage may, for example, believe her daughter has violated the centuries-old codes of society and God. The mother of the young man, by contrast, may be pleased her son now has a place with a clean bath.

It's a rough moment, though, when a woman first breaks it to her parents that she's moving in with a man. They didn't realise you *knew* any men. They just remember the little girl in pigtails who refused to attend Thomas Leach's sixth birthday party on the grounds that 'boy's are yucky', and they are staggered to discover that twenty years later you have revised your view.

Certainly your father is horrified. He knows what young men are like. He used to be one. And he knows they are only interested in one thing. Which is not the clean bath.

Your mother has a different approach. She believes in the need for romance, it's just she can't quite understand why any woman would willingly give up her freedom in order to double her work-load. That's the thing about your mother: she realises that men want sex — and a clean bath.

Blokes' School

But times have changed — and you're confident that with a little bit of encouragement, you and your partner can disprove your mother's old-fashioned and pessimistic assumptions about men. After all, the real-life Prince Charming does not usually arrive on a white charger, bearing a bunch of red roses and a pump-pack of all-purpose cleaner. The perfect live-in partner is not born; he's made.

In other words, you're going to have to put this bloke through a crash course at Blokes' School — a place where the domestically impaired can be introduced to a gleaming new world: a brave new world where sheets are changed more than seasonally, where T-shirts are ironed on both sides, and where shopping isn't always done by one's mum.

There's only one drawback about Blokes' School, and it's that you're the head teacher. And this can be tough for the nineties woman, who may have herself decided that housework is far from fascinating. Indeed many women have spent the last decade carving out a career just so they can avoid it.

That's the harsh reality of many modern partnerships: two totally messy, domestically disinterested people attempting to run a household without any major outbreaks of notifiable disease. And — between the two of you — what ignorance there is! You stand in the kitchen staring blankly at each other, pondering the existential questions of your new life together: exactly how *do* you tell when the meat's gone off? how *do* you unblock a drain? and is your bloke right when he reckons it'll be 'pretty safe' to bung the frozen chook straight into the oven?

You don't have the foggiest, and neither does he.

At least modern manufacturers realise that today's couples aren't strong in the area of domestic knowledge, and are releasing products like Once Over and Spray N' Wipe — in which the name cunningly contains a brief idiot's guide to its use. And how long can it be before the release of a floor cleaner called 'Add Water and Then Scrub the Yucky Bits'?

With the help of such products — and a few tough lessons in Blokes' School — it may even be that you get used to living together, enjoying the sensations of a life spent together: the conversation in the evening, the snuggling up at night and, of course, first thing in the morning, the hot flush upon your cheek of Sargey-Boy's breath.

Maybe this is the man for you. But there's only one way to tell if you're destined to become a married couple — and that's whether you can survive a really good, professional argument.

Which brings us to Chapter Three.

CHAPTER THREE

ARGUING FOR BEGINNERS

or The Six Sorts of Sorry

"Experienced couples know that arguing is not about how you play the game, it's about winning — even if that means dredging up, over and over again, that same adolescent conviction for fare evasion."

So here it is: the big day. With the help of your new bloke, you are about to enjoy your first real stand-up screaming match. Naturally you're nervous. Will it go well? Have you picked the right subject? Have you selected the appropriate ammunition? And most important, is anything off limits — the size of his nose, the morals of his ex-girlfriend, or Sargey-Boy's noisy sexual dysfunction?

Of course, this being your first fight, you'll both be treading carefully. No way are you going to let this degenerate into the sort of endless argument your parents had — 48 hours of solid brawling just to decide who over-fertilised the daphne. *You're* going to keep to the topic in hand, and remember your deep respect for each other. And so it begins:

> *You:* Darling, would you mind shifting your sandshoes off the kitchen bench?
> *Him:* Of course — just as long as you don't ask in that tone.
> *You:* What tone?
> *Him:* There! You're doing it again! Just like your mother.
> *You:* Well, at least *my* mother doesn't have a drinking problem.

Congratulations! First time at it, and already you're arguing like an experienced couple — moving in just a few elegant steps from a simple request to the grounds for divorce. You'd never realised it was so easy.

Already you've stumbled upon the secret of starting an eighteen-round argument. As with lighting a good fire, it's best to start with small kindling and save the big logs for later in the night.

Consider, for example, this popular five-step example:

> *She:* Excuse me darling, do I look fat in this dress?
> *He:* No, you look great.
> *She:* But surely I look a little fat from behind.
> *He:* No, no ... well, maybe just a little.
> *She:* (*Sobs*) Bastard! I might be fat, but at least *I* got my Leaving Certificate.

Note the free exchange of ideas as these two experienced combatants clamber from topic to topic with a wonderfully liberal application of the rules of logic. Here are examples of lateral thinking which would leave even Edward de Bono bewildered.

But there is one strict rule operating in these seemingly random battles: with each exchange of fire the argument must always get worse. As in the classic example:

> *She:* Darling, could you make the salad dressing?
> *He:* What? Just so you're free to ring up your old boyfriends?
> *She:* Well, at least *my* best friend isn't in jail.

With a great start like that, think where you'll be by midnight. Especially as you haven't even started in on his extensive family.

Remember, in the correct hands almost anything can spark a damn good barney. Consider these provocative opening shots — surely enough to cause a brawl in any *normal* marriage:

ARGUING FOR BEGINNERS

> Did you sleep well, darling?
> The garden's looking lovely, sweetheart.
> Have you seen my car keys?
> What's for dinner?
> Where's today's paper?
> Oh. Did the baby wake up last night?

Experienced couples know that arguing is not about how you play the game, it's about winning — even if that means dredging up over and over again that same adolescent conviction for fare evasion. Or that same indiscretion with Christine from work. This is the point about arguing — every spot fire should be doused with diesel fuel. And every wound rubbed with salt.

But surely the worst moment in any marital war of words comes mid screaming match when your bloke manages to land an argument which is — how can we put this? — hurtfully accurate. Suddenly a disturbing and startling thought dawns: maybe he's right. Your behaviour tonight *has* been unforgivable.

You must act quickly. You decide to follow the advice of modern psychotherapy and get in touch with the child inside you. You do. And she's having a screaming tantrum.

It looks as though, in a final burst of desperation, you're going to be forced to resort to some totally meaningless phrases, the sort of meaningless phrases which are heard from seasoned arguers all around the world — especially when they are about to lose the fight:

> Ha! That's rich coming from you.
> Well, excuse me, Mr Perfect.
> Okay, okay, I'm wrong — I'm *always* wrong.
> I think you must have some sort of problem.
> It's not my fault if you're paranoid.
> No wonder mum said I shouldn't marry you.
> etc. etc. etc.

• THE JOY OF BLOKES •

The novice should also be aware that during arguments people say the opposite of what they mean. They say 'I'm sorry' when they're not; they say 'I don't care what you think' when they desperately do; they say 'Okay, I'm wrong' when they're totally convinced they're right, and they say '*You* started it' when in their heart of hearts they know this is a team event.

But don't ever feel limited by a lack of words. For a start, there's always the option of communicating with your partner via the medium of airborne crockery. Or with the help of his new car.

After all, he may deserve it — especially if he's one of those blokes who in mid-argument resorts to unpleasantly inflected muttering. You can't quite understand the words, but it doesn't sound good:

> *She:* Come on, admit it — you've got a thing about my friends.
> *He:* I never said that.
> *She:* What *did* you say then?
> *He:* (*exiting room, spluttering to himself*): Fargggh barrvgh ratchitz brajket wodge fidget klaatch thrumprawt blzzkt!
> *She:* (*hot on his trail*) *What* did you say?
> *He:* (*innocently*) Nothing darling, nothing at all.

Like any competitive event, the main thing is practice, practice, practice. And that means not only celebrating the anniversary of your marriage or first date, but also honouring the anniversaries of your most memorable fights. Indeed, experienced couples may even find time to re-enact them — as in this marvellous effort performed annually by Judy and Jeff Barton, of Shanks Ave, Curtin, ACT:

> *She:* Darling, do you realise it's exactly three years today since we had that horrible fight about fixing the shower door?

He: No it's not. It's only two years.
She: It's not!
He: YES, IT IS!
She: Next you'll be saying you're over that infatuation with Leanne.
He: At least Leanne can drive without grinding the gears.

Well done, Judy and Jeff. Mmm, there's nothing like a happy anniversary.

CHOOSING THE ARGUMENT THAT'S BEST FOR YOU

In order to sustain a relationship of variety and spice, you may find it necessary to experiment with a wide variety of arguments. We can only recommend:

The Hunt-the-problem Argument

Both partners enter the room, at which point the woman adopts a look of total misery.

He: What's the matter, darling?
She: I can't believe you don't know.
He: Was it something I said, or something I did?
She: I'm just staggered you're so insensitive.

The man then spends the rest of the day trailing behind his distressed wife, begging for hints, in the later stages having recourse to such techniques as 'Is it animal, vegetable or mineral?' and 'Just give me the letter it starts with.'

The Trying-to-remember-what-you-were-arguing-about Argument

The argument has been raging for some hours, when the inevitable happens and he says sulkily:

> *He:* Well, you started it!
> *She:* How dare you blame me! It was you that started it!

Sure, you can remember him accusing you of throwing out his old *Mad* magazines. But was that before or after you accused him of spilling coffee grounds on your second semester essay?

And besides, who was it that accused the other of having a borderline personality disorder? The reality is that this argument has been going for so long it's unlikely that anybody can remember who started it. Except, of course, those lucky people next door. And they think you've *both* got personality disorders.

The Reading-between-the-lines Argument

This is a form of arguing for those repressed couples who find it difficult to express their true feelings. That's why they have to communicate by reading between the lines. For example:

He: Why do we always have to buy the spirally spaghetti when I like the little tubes?

(Meaning: I've been having a wild affair at the office for the past year, and now I want out of this sham of a marriage.)

She: Okay, Graeme, I'll get the little tubes.

(Meaning: Go stick your pasta where the sun never shines. By the time my divorce lawyer's finished with you, spaghetti will be all you can afford.)

The Trying-to-end-the-argument Argument

Beginning an argument is simple; ending it is tougher. Especially since, with proper effort from both sides, the acrimonious peace negotiations can be so much more extensive than the argument itself. Who, for example, hasn't had experience with this classic?

He: (*sulkily*) I've already made one overture to end this, and you rejected it.
She: (*acidly*) I did not.
He: Yes you did!
She: No I didn't!
He: Did so — and now it's your turn to say sorry.
She: Already have!
He: Did not ...
She: At least *my* father wasn't a golf cheat.

But this is nothing compared to the open warfare that occurs when you start discussing precisely *how* each of you should say sorry. Or as it is officially called:

• THE JOY OF BLOKES •

The Saying-sorry-properly Argument

This is a popular variant on the traditional argument, 'It's not what you said it's the way that you said it'. As any experienced bloke knows, 'sorry' is a word of rich ambiguity. Delivered with the correct inflection of injured truculence it can be turned into the most potent of insults, causing normally forgiving women to reach for the meat axe.

Particularly popular among blokes is:

• **The Barely-audible Sorry** — which is where the word is mumbled rapidly and with virtually no trace of sincerity directly into a coat stand.

• **The Forced Sorry** — in which the alleged apology is squeezed out through gritted teeth as if you were at that very moment strapping electrodes to his private parts. Which, when you come think about it, is not such a bad idea.

• **The Shifty Sorry** — an apology which even your bloke himself doesn't really believe, which may be why his eyes are scanning the carpet in an attempt to disguise his patent lack of sincerity. This is not the sort of sorry which emerges when he realises how wrong he was. It's the sort of sorry which emerges when he realises that it's 7.30 pm and he doesn't want to miss the start of *Roseanne*.

• **The Screamed Sorry** — this is not an apology, it's an outside broadcast. This is the 'sorry' where your bloke stands at the top of the steps, his face red with rage, the veins on his neck throbbing, bellowing like a bullock in its death throes, 'Okay, I'm sorry!!!!' And somehow you, and the rest of the neighbourhood, get the feeling that all is not quite forgiven.

• **The Conditional Sorry** — this is possibly the most popular 'sorry' of all. 'I'm sorry,' your bloke will say boldly, pausing just a moment before whispering the poisoned conditional clause, 'I'm very sorry if *you* took it that way.' Of course, according to your bloke, only a total imbecile *would* take it that way. And yes, he *is* sorry — sorry that you haven't yet apologised.

• **The Patronising Sorry** — this 'sorry' is said with feigned sweetness and an oily charm — as if your bloke has deigned to calm a deranged child. 'I am so sorry …' he'll say in the quiet voice which a senior psychiatrist would use when explaining why he needs to increase your dose. The patronising sorry is not only worse than no sorry at all, it's also grounds for divorce.

DANGER ZONES

— A Word of Caution

Arguments are all part of a healthy marriage, but there remain certain topics risked by only the most foolhardy of couples. These are the danger zones.

Photographic appreciation

She: Why are you looking at that Elle Macpherson calender?
He: I'm just curious about the exact date of South Australian Proclamation day.
She: You think Elle's more attractive than me, don't you?

• THE JOY OF BLOKES •

He: I never said that.
She: But you're thinking it.
He: Darling, I think you're witty and warm and a really great mum to the kids.
She: Go on, admit it! You think she's more physically attractive than me.
He: Well … ummm … it's like this …

☞ BLOKES! STOP! THINK! YOU HAVE JUST ENTERED THE DANGER ZONE!

Liking his friends a little too much

She: Is your mate George coming around tonight?
He: Why do you ask?
She: Well, he's a good bloke.
He: What do you mean, 'good bloke'?
She: He's funny and intelligent and … I suppose he's also quite good looking.
He: What do you mean, 'good looking'?
She: Come on, Peter, I think it's pretty bloody obvious. George is just this incredible spunk.

☞ WOMEN! STOP! THINK! YOU HAVE JUST ENTERED THE DANGER ZONE!

• ARGUING FOR BEGINNERS •

Searching for clues

She: Notice anything different about me?
He: (*unconvincingly*) Ummm ... Ye-es.
She: Well, go on, tell me ...
He: It's your hair ... it's all different ...
She: (*coldly*) It's been like this for two years.
He: (*examining her desperately*) Oh. Yes, of course. I know! Ummm, in that case it's your ...

☞BLOKES! STOP! THINK! YOU HAVE JUST ENTERED THE DANGER ZONE!

Bedtime stories

She: Darling, you were fantastic ... the best ...
He: (*preening*) Oh, so you're finally admitting I'm better than Sean?
She: You leave my ex out of this. He wasn't that bad.
He: What do you mean?
She: Oh, don't be so juvenile. I'm not about to start comparing you.
He: Ha! I bet there wasn't even one thing he did better.
She: (*wistfully*) Well, maybe just one thing ...

☞WOMEN! STOP! THINK! YOU HAVE JUST ENTERED THE DANGER ZONE!

• THE JOY OF BLOKES •

Video shop amnesia

She: Let's get *Die Hard 2*.
He: But we've already seen it.
She: No we haven't.
He: Yes we have. You remember — at the motel.
She: What motel?
He: The one with the vibrating bed. You loved it!
She: (*icily*) I've never been near a vibrating bed!
He: Yes, you have ... no, oops, wait a minute ...

☞ BLOKES! STOP! THINK! YOU HAVE JUST ENTERED THE DANGER ZONE

And, since we are talking about danger zones, what better time to shift chapters and move on to a particularly delicate subject, a subject which lies at the heart of the modern debate over the hegemonic role of patriarchy in determining gender roles in Judeo-Christian culture.

Or, to put it another way, how come men never, ever, clean the toilet?

CHAPTER FOUR

STUNT HOUSEWORK

and the Trial of Somebody

"He's only interested in the big jobs. The flashy jobs. The show-off jobs. He's interested in *Stunt* Housework. Housework in front of an audience. Housework that creates a lot of noise. Housework he can brag about later. Housework that involves a ladder. And most crucially, housework that only needs doing every leap year."

The official statistics show that men now do 30 per cent of the nation's housework, leaving women all over Australia pondering the bewildering question: how did the figure come to be so high? The answer is Stunt Housework.

For 364 days a year, your partner is a champion at avoiding his share. But then — on the Second Sunday of Spring, when the full moon is high — he finally stirs from the couch and starts conducting his annual review of the state of the house.

And he's very, very disappointed with what he finds. While he had his mind on more important things, you've allowed *his* house to slump into squalor. And there's only one thing for it: he'll have to step in and, as usual, fix the lot himself — all in one afternoon.

Not that he's interested in doing the tedious, regular jobs like cleaning the toilet, doing the ironing or putting the clothes away. Oh, no. *Anyone* can do that. For instance *you*.

He's only interested in the big jobs. The flashy jobs. The show-off jobs. He's interested in *Stunt* Housework.

Housework in front of an audience. Housework that creates a lot of noise. Housework he can brag about later. Housework that involves a ladder. And most crucially, housework that only needs doing every leap year.

He's the Red Adair of home duties — and he only responds to major league assignments, like washing down the venetians, reordering the record collection, cleaning out the light fittings or scouring grease on the exhaust fan.

And — like any stunt show — there's a running commentary.

'*Who* let the venetians get this filthy?' '*Who* bought this many tinned tomatoes?' '*Who* could endure the squalor of this cupboard?' and 'Honestly, I think this kitchen is a rats' paradise.'

With a superior snort he locates a packet of desiccated coconut with a use-by date in the mid 1980s. He's so appalled he even considers — fleetingly — becoming involved in the running of the household.

Quickly he comes to his senses. Red Adair don't do no shopping. But he *is* going to fix up the bathroom — once and for all. And by late afternoon he's unpacked the medicine cabinet, unscrewed the exhaust fan, dismantled the toilet for cleaning, removed the shower curtain and is halfway through installing a dimmer on the light.

And that's when he notices the tennis has started.

It's going to be a great match. Especially if he treats himself to a beer or two. 'Don't worry,' he says, stretching out on the lounge. 'I'll finish up later.'

Sure he will. Maybe next year. On the Second Sunday of Spring, when the full moon is once again high.

Erogenous Zones

So, how *do* you get a man to do his share, and go beyond mere Stunt Housework? Forget all those arguments of logic and justice and interpersonal responsibility. You've got to use words that will capture his attention, and that means one thing:

SEX

• STUNT HOUSEWORK •

There, bet he's paying attention now. Basically your bloke has got to be re-educated about your major erogenous zones. After all, he still thinks they are your nipples, thighs and ear-lobes. Whereas what really needs a steamy rub-down is your filthy kitchen floor.

There's been much talk recently about aphrodisiacs, and whether they really work. But for the busy nineties woman it's just not an issue: there's only one thing that really gets her going — and that's the sight of her husband, bending over in a pair of shortie pyjamas, buttocks waggling and thighs clenched, as he scrubs the kitchen floor. And to most women this isn't housework. This is foreplay.

But, of course, no reasonable woman can make her partner spend *all* night scrubbing the kitchen floor.

Not when he's still got to defrost the fridge, scrape the grilled cheese off the griller, and get rid of all the little chunks of meat and rice that have got stuck in the sink strainer.

Thank goodness that later on in the evening your man will still be able to go wild and follow his animal instincts: giving a real hose-out to the Kitty Litter tray. Certainly, it's fantastic when he does it. And somehow sex never seems so messy, not when your man reeks of Pine-O-Clean.

That's the thing about a lot of men: they don't realise how women can be erotically affected by the sight of a man ironing. 'Who needs Iron John?' as various feminists have put it. 'It's an Ironing John *we're* after.' Here, after all, is the one plug-in appliance which, when used by a man, is guaranteed to leave a woman crying for more — as well as with a full rack of neatly pressed office wear.

That's why men are so gullible when they fill in those magazine ads for pheromones — the spray-on female-attractant which promises to make dating easy.

They'd do better by far to save their $44.95, and instead try a far more effective attractant: that subtle smell of the Sensitive New Age Guy, achieved by a quick squirt of Fabulon behind the ears.

Just like the pheromones, the incredible Fabulon works on a woman's subconscious — without her knowing why. Amazingly, she won't understand why she wants to leave the restaurant, clutching the man's arm, breathing in the heady scent.

Nor, when the man gets her home, will she understand quite why she's behaving so rashly: suddenly removing all her clothes, throwing them dramatically in the corner, and begging the bloke, in her throatiest voice, to gently launder them all.

It's the power of Fabulon — the scent of a *real* man.

Yet some men still persist with the idea that housework is women's work; and weirdest of all are the macho men who have this strict code about the jobs it's okay for a real man to do. Cleaning out the gutters is okay; cleaning out the shower recess is wussy. Cleaning window glass is okay (if it involves going squirt-squirt with a pump-pack with a trigger); but cleaning a drinking glass is for girls.

It's like old-style unionism, full of strange demarcation disputes. These blokes are The Amalgamated Avoiders and Delegators.

The Amalgamated Avoiders will change the light bulb, but they'll steadfastly refuse to wipe any dead moths out of the shade. That's a gazetted job for the Guild of Womenfolk. The Avoiders might drill a hole, but it's more than their job is worth to vacuum up the mess. *That's* for the Womenfolk.

Is there any answer to this particular demarcation dispute? Like any industrial battle, you may need to go on strike — and a strike which will hit them where it hurts. Which brings us back to where we started:

• STUNT HOUSEWORK •

SEX

As a nineties woman, you've got to speak out about your real needs and desires. And that's why *The Joy of Blokes* recommends industrial action — introducing your bloke to the iron and its power point, all the while repeating the famous slogan: 'If it's not on, it's not on.'

Ah, housework — it's how to satisfy a woman every single time.

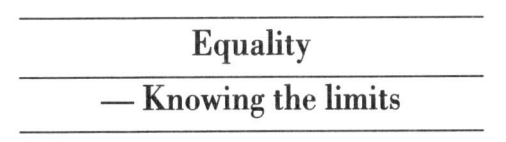

Equality
— Knowing the limits

As a modern woman you will no doubt want to insist on the most thorough standards of household equality — even if you do end up becoming a Lysistrata of the pots and pans. But in your feminist zeal it *is* possible to go too far.

For instance, it is important not to end up with a man who has lost all his male dignity, and is left without the merest spark of machismo. And that's why women — including those who practice weightlifting — often request their bloke's help in prising open the lid of a stubborn gherkin jar. And how marvellous it is to witness the absurd amount of pleasure such a simple act can bring to the average slump-shouldered, work-defeated, spiritually troubled bloke — suddenly turning him into a temple of testosterone, a Claude Van Damme, just glowing with contented pride.

Indeed, it's a little known fact that when a man has a sperm test and is asked to bring a jar, it's just so he can first prove his virility by prising it open in front of the female receptionist.

Yet the modern male does not need to rest his whole sense of self on this ability to provide gherkin in times of need. There's another job which even the toughest feminist is happy to define as a job for the boys, however intense her belief in equal rights.

It's up to men to kill all vermin. And that's that.

There will be no further discussion on this matter.

Australia's Most Wanted

The removal of vermin isn't the only thing you'll have to consider when living with a man. You'll also have to come to terms with the uninvited guest who suddenly appears to have moved into your house.

It happens whenever a man and a woman live together — a mysterious third party enters their relationship. It is a person who eats at their table, sleeps in their bed and at night, when no one is up, rifles through their personal effects.

This stranger is a hardened criminal, a repeat offender with a heart as black as a raven.

It is that evil doer that men call 'somebody'. And every day men plaintively catalogue 'somebody's' life of crime. *Somebody's* stolen my car keys. *Somebody's* broken the video. *Somebody's* forgotten to renew the car insurance.

Since there's only the two of you in the house, it's unclear exactly who he means — but it seems *you're* the one who needs an alibi. In fact, a few alibis — because somebody's certainly been busy.

No wonder your bloke feels victimised. He gets up in the morning — after a long night in which 'somebody' has been hogging the doona — and then it's off to the bathroom where 'somebody' has blunted his razor and 'somebody' has used his towel. And there's no rest for the wicked. According to your bloke's charge sheet, 'somebody' has also eaten the last of the raisin toast, left the milk out to spoil, misappropriated his wallet, pilfered his favourite comb and then wilfully shifted the biro from its special place next to the phone.

'Somebody's got it in for me,' he cries.

She's unstoppable, reprehensible and unscrupulous, this 'somebody'. But god, you've got to admit it, you admire her style.

And even more amazing, when you talk to your girlfriends you realise the scope of her work: 'somebody' has been busy creating this sort of havoc for every man in the country.

It's a tough job, but *somebody's* got to do it ... just like sex.

Roll on Chapter Five.

CHAPTER FIVE

SEX

The Eternal Triangle (You, Him and Sharon Stone)

"These days it's considered healthy for you both to have sexual fantasies. He might want to pretend that you are Sharon Stone. And you might want to pretend that he's done the washing-up. Both are rich and satisfying fantasies — just as long as neither of you lose touch with reality and believe they are actually true."

So here you are: lying in bed with your partner, clothes strewn through the house, an empty champagne bottle rolling on the floor, the doona kicked off and the phone off the hook. It's either the throes of passion or you're just very, very bad housekeepers.

Hopefully it's the passion, because sex is one of the very best reasons to have a bloke around. The Aussie bloke may vary in his ability to bolt a clothes dryer to a wall, whip up a spaghetti carbonara or fix a stuffed diff. But the vast majority find it pretty difficult to say no to a woman, especially when she's wearing nothing but a clingy nightdress and a warm smile.

Yet at some stage even the most sexually compatible couple will suffer some sort of sexual problem, and there's one male problem that stands out pretty clearly. Or rather doesn't. And before we mention its name, it might be a good idea to clear all blokes from the vicinity — just in case they peer over your shoulder, see what you are reading, and irreversible damage is caused.

And of course the problem we are talking about — have they gone yet? — the problem is impotence. And the fear of impotence is *so* great among men that a man can become impotent just by seeing it written out. Like this: IMPOTENT. Or even like this: *I M P O T E N T*. Or even in a non-threatening, very small italic like this: *impotent*.

And no matter how fleeting the problem, it has to be treated with enormous sensitivity. After all, your bloke will be convinced he's no longer attracted by women; he'll be convinced this means he's gay; and he'll be convinced that you're going to workshop his problem with all your girlfriends, probably over a couple of rounds of margaritas.

His mind is beset by a million fears, and he's wrong about them all. All except the workshopping with your girlfriends, and that can wait until tomorrow.

Right now he needs reassurance. Tell him you understand. Tell him this problem happens to all men. Tell him it doesn't mean he's gay. Tell him anything — just as long as he stops badgering you about what he should wear to the next Mardi Gras.

To your bloke it all seems so utterly unfair. He spent his adolescence *plagued* by erections — all of them appearing when no formal invitation had been issued. There was the time during Ms Stetson's maths class when for some reason differential calculus became suddenly arousing. There was that time on the diving highboard at the state swimming championships, when he switched mid-air from a pike to a tuck. And perhaps most embarrassing of all, there was his unexpectedly intense reaction when body-searched by French customs officials.

But now it's party time — the invitation has been offered and accepted but the guest of honour has failed to turn up. It's nature's cruel joke: *you've* just reached your sexual peak, and *he* was willing and able two decades ago. And so now your bloke is *trying* to think sexy thoughts. He's *straining* to think sexy thoughts. Thoughts about the gentle curve of your body, the alluring sway of your body under your silk chemise, the swell of your breasts ... the swell of anybody's breasts.

But each thought does a U-turn in the dark alley of his mind, and your bloke is left staring at the flashing neon sign.

IMPOTENT. IMPOTENT. IMPOTENT.

All through a bloke's life, the penis and the brain have been locked in mortal combat, but now — suddenly — these two crucial male organs have swapped roles. It's the brain which is saying, 'Come on, baby, let's have some fun,' and the world-weary penis which is sighing and groaning, 'Come on, buddy, give it a rest. We're not 19 any longer.'

It's a bleak moment for any man. After all, men are *supposed* to be lust-crazed animals, wanting to spread their seed with all the discretion of a crop-duster. But now the crop-duster is in the hangar, the ignition is dead, and even jump-starting won't get this baby heading skywards.

And why wouldn't your bloke be tired? Today's man is exhausted. He's playing more roles than Anthony Hopkins. And he's expected to be able to do everything — from bolting in the clothes dryer with a shifting spanner, to earning a wage, right through to discussing his deep-seated feelings while mixing up a cheeky little vinaigrette. No wonder sometimes he can't get it up. The clothes dryer that is.

Just give him love, understanding, and maybe a new shifting spanner. And never, ever, mention the I-word.

The Speed Demons

But impotence isn't the only male sexual problem. Most men, for instance, are highly competitive beings, and will often compete with their partners to be the first to complete many ordinary household tasks, such as orgasm.

For these men, seduction may involve stroking your cheek, caressing your waist and promising: 'Darling, I can give you the best 15 seconds of your life.'

If you want to avoid such types, watch for the warning signs, such as men who suggest sex during a commercial break or while their breakfast egg is boiling. These are the blokes who as kids could never wait to open their Christmas presents.

Today nothing's changed. It's nice to have someone find you attractive but frankly it would be nice if he could wait until you are in the same room.

Faking It

But other men may have the opposite problem, and you may be shocked to find that your bloke has been faking it for years. He may, for instance, be constantly telling you that you haven't put on any weight, that he likes your new hair colour, and that no, under no circumstances, would he sleep with Winona Ryder — even if she begged him.

Fantasy Land

These days it's considered healthy for you both to have sexual fantasies. He might want to pretend that you are Sharon Stone. And you might want to pretend that he's done the washing-up. Both are rich and satisfying fantasies — just as long as neither of you lose touch with reality and believe they are actually true.

Or you may decide to make a fantasy come true. Many couples, for instance, have spiced up their sex lives by making love in an exotic location, such as inside their wheely bin or behind some filing cabinets at the Vatican. And, according to one official report, 72.1 per cent of Australian men have at some time wanted to make love while wearing a false Merv Hughes moustache. Who can blame them? *We* think it's sexy.

Three per cent, on the other hand, have reached satisfaction while daydreaming that they are being disciplined by the Deputy Commissioner of Taxation, Mr D.J. Cortese. Apparently he's just fabulous. And the rest of the male population are just normal red-blooded blokes who like to imagine they are having a slow, languid afternoon in bed with the entire cast of *Keeping Up Appearances*.

Certainly, your bloke may wish to really break new ground in ex-

• SEX •

ploring his own sexuality. And the night may well come when he draws you into an embrace and announces that from now on he'll be batting for the other side. Don't panic. This may simply mean that he has recently secured a position opening for the West Indies.

THE FEMALE FWOOAR

But in the nineties women are also becoming more confident about expressing their sexuality — largely because at last they've been allowed to have one. And to admit that just sometimes they find a passing man attractive.

In decades past, both sexes were in agreement on one point: that the male body was, by its very nature, unattractive. Women were there to be leered at; men weren't. And society agreed that the penis and testicles were ridiculous things of no aesthetic appeal.

These days, however, all these ideas have been discarded as part of a total reappraisal of the male body. Except, of course, for the testicles, which remain ridiculous.

But hot-blooded women everywhere are working at redressing the balance. As in the past, they still appreciate a man's dark, flashing eyes and his aquiline nose. But now it's also worth trying to cop an eyeful of his washboard stomach and muscular bum. The female *Fwooar* has arrived.

There are the football calenders. The live shows. The risque talk in the ladies room. And a lot of very nervous men.

And can we be surprised that the Aussie bloke is flinching under this sudden scrutiny? Suddenly he is expected to measure up — which can be tough when his partner comes armed with a ruler and a Manpower calender. Which is why, just sometimes, Aussie men dream of society returning to the good old days — a time when only the local baker would have his buns ogled.

Women *are* more open about admitting an interest in sex but — let's be honest — they've still got some way to go before they catch up with men.

It's not that men think about sex all the time. Sometimes they think about the cigarette *after* sex. Or having a drink *before* sex. But sex is the centrepiece of the bloke psyche. He talks about it constantly (which is called oral sex). And he *thinks* about it, on average, once every twelve minutes. Even more when he's awake.

You watch a scientist halfway through an experiment that could change the future of humanity. What's in the front of his mind? Sex. Or your bloke's in the dentist's chair having root canal therapy. The minute the drill stops, what's his first thought? Sex.

Not that a bloke fancies everyone. He's got standards. To attract him a person has to be both female and alive.

Of course these days the blatant objectification — the whistling and cat calling — is beginning to disappear. Or at least be left to the women. But the male obsession continues. The brain may be sensitive, pro-feminist and aware. But the female breast, encased in a tight jumper, or straining against a silk shirt, appears to have its own irresistible magnetic force.

And according to your bloke, he's just got to look; the eyes are drawn without reference to the brain. And the best he can hope for is not to be caught in the act of ogling.

And so the leer is going underground, as each man develops his own repertoire of Post-Feminist, Secretive, Subtle Gawps. And it's time modern women were warned of the Sensitive New Age Oglers in their midst. Just cast your eye over this widely researched list — and next time you are out in public, be well prepared:

• SEX •

The March Past

A popular nineties technique, used by New Age Oglers right at the moment they are about to cross paths with a woman. To have a squiz as she strides into sight would of course be offensive, rude, old-fashioned, patriarchal and downright obvious. And that's why, with great consideration, the reconstructed man lowers his eyes to the pavement as the woman walks towards him. Right until the last critical moment. Then he cops an eyeful. Fwooar.

The Rubbernecker

A dangerous stunt technique, performed by men caught in the act of a quick goggle in the office. Suddenly, brutally, the man twists his neck upwards, away from the woman's eyeline — feigning an urgent interest in that air-conditioning duct above her desk. Indeed, in this era of secretive leers, women may be wondering why so many of their male colleagues have developed such an unflagging fascination with the science of air-conditioning. And why so many are wearing a surgical neck brace.

Shark Patrol

No way is the modern man going to be caught admiring the bikinis on the beach, like those sexist deadheads of the past. Instead, he and his mate are standing in the shallows, arms folded, allegedly keeping an eye out for sharks. And, behind their sunglasses they are indeed on the lookout for a couple of white pointers. It was for gawpers like this they invented the summer slogan 'slip, slop, slap'.

Gyms

The blokes say they are going to gym to increase their heart rate, and they're right, and that's without even doing the class. Best of all, the women usually don't notice when they're having a look. *They* are too busy checking out the pecs on the guys with the free weights.

Mr Dropsie

It used to be that women dropped a handkerchief and men picked it up. Now it's men dropping anything, all over the place, just so they can get down there on floor level and really check out your ankles. Mr Dropsie is the lowest form of life — whenever he gets the chance.

Not Drowning, Perving

Swimming laps can be a boring form of exercise — except for those blokes willing to attempt this high-speed precision perve. The man is ploughing up the pool; in the next lane, a woman is plowing along in the opposite direction. And there's just one millisecond when — by carefully timing his intake of breath — he can also cop a quick goggleful. Not to mention a lungful of water. It is the act of a desperate man. And is it really worth it when his next stroke's straight into the wall?

Backwards Glance

Of all the advances of modern technology, surely the swivelling electric side-mirror is the closest to the gawker's heart. He spots a woman

· SEX ·

in the car behind. Suddenly Bzzzzzzz. The side-mirrors are on red alert. Oh, and another good sort, just behind, on the inside lane. Bzzzzzzzzzz. A woman on the pavement. Bzz. But this is ogling at its most dangerous. Especially when, minutes later, he is halfway through a high speed overtake and suddenly all he can see in his side-mirrors is tree tops and sky. Bzz. Bz. Crash.

All in all, a woman has got to go through a lot in order to survive the world of sex, and emerge with a suitable father for her children. But, take heart. At least when men become fathers, women usually get to see them at their pretty-near best ... which is the cue for Chapter Six.

CHAPTER SIX

FATHERHOOD

The New Man in Action

"The *Kama Sutra for Parents* is not so much a book as a very flimsy pamphlet — and it starts by ruling out all those passionate sounds of love-making: the moaning, the panting, the thrilling 'oohhhhhhhhhh'. For parents there's only one word normally associated with orgasm, and that's 'Shhhhh!' "

You've enjoyed the sex and you've got the child. And suddenly you've got to tell your bloke the truth: that most women don't feel like sex for a while after giving birth.

'That's fine,' he'll say, supportively. 'I wouldn't mind a few days' rest myself.' After all, he's learnt all about Tantric Sex, in which men learn to delay the moment of their orgasm for hours at a time. What he doesn't realise is that this time around he'll be delaying his orgasm for around eight or nine months.

After you break the news, try to ignore the look of unabashed incredulity on his ashen face. 'Nine months of celibacy,' he'll stammer, shaken to the core. 'It's impossible to conceive.' Yes! You've got to admit he's got a point.

But it's not all the fault of your hormones. You've just given birth — and the new baby is not only adorable, gurgling and button-nosed; he's also a fast-growing contraceptive device.

Children make it virtually impossible to have a normal sex life with your bloke. They seem to have a built-in antenna, and they just *know* the moment you've rolled over in bed and whispered amorously into your bloke's ears: 'How about it, sweetie-pie?'

Two rooms away, through a shut door and double-brick construction, a pair of little ears twitch. Something is not right in this household. Something is seriously amiss. He's not sure what. But urgent action must be taken. *Whack* go the feet on the ground. *Thump* goes his bedroom door. *Boom-boom-boom-boom-boom* go the feet, pounding up the hallway. And *Whoooosh* goes his body, airborne as he flies toward the bed, and scores a direct hit, mid-doona, right between the two of you.

The game is up. Like a well-trained fireman, he's spotted the smoke, launched into action, and doused the flames of passion — all before any real heat was generated. 'Hi, Mummy, what are you doing?'

'Nothing, darling,' you mumble, 'Well, not any more ...'

Why does your child behave in this extraordinarily perceptive way? Following months of experiments, scientists now believe he may be displaying an extremely advanced form of sibling rivalry. Not only is he going to stop his pesky sibling playing with *his* Lego, he's even going to stop the kid being conceived.

So how *do* you make love with your bloke after the first child is born? The answer is very quickly, very quietly, and very, very late at night. The *Kama Sutra for Parents* is not so much a book as a very flimsy pamphlet — and it starts by ruling out all those passionate sounds of love-making: the moaning, the panting, the thrilling 'oohhhhhhhhhh'. For parents there's only one word normally associated with orgasm, and that's 'Shhhhh!'

Of course, all the standard components of love-making are still there. There's the well-practised foreplay ('Hey, give me a hand latching the door'). There's the whispered longings ('Hurry up Greg'). And finally there's that very special moment just before climax, when a throaty voice mumbles in your ear: 'Mummy, can I have a glass of water?'

Your secret midnight plan — *Mission: Ignite Passion* — has failed once again.

So how do strict Catholics end up with ten children? Search us. We can only imagine it's something to do with the rhythm method. And that they put on dance tracks so loud they can't even hear the cries for water.

The rest of us must do the best we can. Even if it means employing our own series of sultry sexual come-on lines. Not 'Do you come here often?' but the alluring 'Quick — *Playschool* ends in fifteen minutes'. Not 'Can I buy you a drink? but the knee-trembling 'Let's drop them off at Grandma's'.

But just occasionally, together in your bed, you'll find sex is still a time for discovering things, things you thought you'd lost long, long ago. Like that Thomas the Tank Engine carriage lodged under your left buttock. And the sharp little Lego bits sticking into your thigh. And Bert and Ernie. And the Blue Teddy. And the complete Scalextric Le Mans race kit.

Who says couples with kids get bored in bed? As a matter of fact, there's plenty to do, including exploring a fascinating ménage à trois with Big Bird. Yes, you may have left the sexy single lifestyle behind, but it's only now that you find your bed is full of battery-operated devices.

Coping with your Bloke as he Copes with Fatherhood

Fatherhood comes as a shock to many men. They can't believe their freedom is over, they can't believe the love they feel for the new infant and, most of all, they can't believe the size of the obstetrician's bill.

It's now, with a small child, that you will really discover the measure of your man. Anyone can appear patient and good-natured when drinking a mai-tai at a singles bar on the Gold Coast; but how will your bloke rate at 3 am, after three sleepless nights up with baby Callum, who's just developed his fourth middle-ear infection of the season?

Fatherhood will change his life irrevocably. Suddenly he'll find himself eating a breakfast cereal he can't stand, just so his child can complete his glow-in-the-dark Butterfly Card collection. Or he'll go to a dinner party — the first in months — and spend all the time arguing with the other parents about who's the best *Playschool* presenter. Or he'll realise that the only song being played on his $2000 sub-woofer car stereo is 'In The Ning Nang Nong Where The Cows Go Bong'.

Still he loves it. For a start, he's finally found someone he can beat at Scrabble, and who believes that 'xerpotz' is a real word.

Dialogues with Daddy

Three years ago this new dad was a hip, broad-minded man-about-town with an interest in acid jazz and current affairs. Now all the news he hears is about Agro's latest colouring competition and how Morgan's sister got a splinter in her bum.

Even more surprising, he's discovering his willpower is no match for that of a sullen and determined three year old. He may be six foot two and an experienced hand at enterprise bargaining, but he can't seem to achieve a settlement on the issue of whether Dominic can spend another ten minutes on the big swings and the thing that goes round and round.

And when it comes to a serious issue, he's completely at sea.

Dominic: Where are we going, Daddy?
Daddy: We're going to see Auntie Jan, mate.
Dominic: Dad, why does Auntie Jan have such a big tummy?
Daddy: Because she has a baby inside it.
Dominic: Why?
Daddy: She just does.
Dominic: Did she eat it?
Daddy: Not exactly.
Dominic: So how did it get in there?
Daddy: Well, Uncle Steve ... um, well Uncle Steve put it in there.
Dominic: How?
Daddy (brusquely): He just did. He's very clever like that.

• FATHERHOOD •

Dominic: But where did *he* get the baby?
Daddy: I don't know. It was just sort of inside him.
Dominic: But how did the baby get *inside* Uncle Steve. Did he eat it?
Daddy: He did no such thing.
Dominic (sobbing): He must of, he must have eaten the baby.
Daddy: Come on, Dom, into the car, we're running late.
Dominic (screaming and weeping): I'm not going! I'm not going! They eat children.
Daddy: Stop it now, Dom!
Dominic (screaming): Mummy, Mummy — Daddy's trying to feed me to the child-eaters.
Mummy (enters): What on earth are you telling him, David! Sometimes I wonder if I can leave you alone with him for a minute.
Daddy (*shamed*): Sorry, darling.

Yet fathers don't spend all the time discussing ludicrous childhood fears. Sometimes they discuss more weighty subjects.

Kid: Dad, who's that on the Christmas card?
Daddy: That's the baby Jesus.
Kid: Where is he now?
Daddy: Well he, er, died and went to heaven.
Kid: My guinea pig Ralph went to heaven.
Daddy: I guess he did.
Kid: And Jesus feeds Ralph, every day in his cage.
Daddy: Possibly.
Kid: Which means Jesus must own a pet food shop.
Daddy: Well, possibly.
Kid: And he uses it to feed the Easter Bunny. And to feed Nana, 'cause she's gone to heaven.
Daddy: Mmmm. Well, mmmm.
Kid (shouting): Mummy! Daddy says Jesus feeds Nana pet food in

heaven and — guess what — she's in the same cage as Ralph.
Mummy (enters): David, are you sane? Why on earth are you filling the poor little child's head with all this bizarre rubbish?
Daddy (shamed): Sorry, darling.

But, of course, when children get just a little older, they can achieve a firmer grip on reality. Firmer, certainly, than that of your beleaguered bloke.

Daddy: Time to go to bed, sweetie.
Isabelle: But I want to watch my *Beauty and the Beast* video.
Daddy: You can't watch a two-hour movie — it's 8 o'clock.
Isabelle: Why not? You do.
Daddy: I'm not discussing this any further. It's bedtime.
Isabelle: But Mummy said I could watch some telly.
Daddy: Well, maybe until the next ad break — then it's clean teeth and into bed.
Isabelle: What about two ad breaks, one more juice, a few songs, and no teeth cleaning?
Daddy: No way, kid. It's two ad breaks, no juice, one song, a cuddle, and a light brush over. And *noooooo* arguments.
Isabelle: The juice is fine, the teeth's okay, but it's no deal without four ad breaks of *Hey, Hey It's Saturday*. Plus you make pancakes for breakfast, with maple syrup and lemon, and the edges all crispy. Yum!
Daddy (shouting): I've had enough. I'm tired. And I will not be ordered about by a five year old. Daddy has worked bloody hard all day. And so has Mummy. And *now* you want pancakes. This is just bloody ridiculous. You get nothing. Nothing. It's bed. Now!
Isabelle: Waaaaahhhhhhhhh.
Mummy (entering): David, calm down. I just don't understand why you want to get her so worked up — and just before her bedtime.
Daddy (shamed): Sorry, darling.

• FATHERHOOD •

Home Alone

With a bit of luck — and a lot of training — you should end up with a newish man: one who will at least *claim* he does half the parenting. This is useful should you ever wish to go away alone on a business trip or a short holiday. Because, however terrified your partner is at the thought of being left alone with the kids, he won't be able to say anything.

After years of proclaiming how he is nobly carrying half the load, he'll be forced to just look up from his paper and say : 'A trip away? Fine, no problems. It'll just be business as usual round here.'

Of course, he's lying.

Inside this seemingly confident exterior your partner is imploding. He's in a state of advanced anxiety. For a start he doesn't want to admit all the things he doesn't know about the household routine. Things like: How much do you pay the babysitter? What time does school finish? And how many children have we got anyway?

But he's determined that you won't see a trace of panic. He's a new man. He'll cope. And he doesn't like to say it, but — actually — he's confident he'll do it better than you ever did. After all, he's a bloke with systems.

And so it starts. The descent into domestic hell.

It begins on the first morning, just when your bloke is halfway through frying up a small sheep. His aim: to make enough lamb casserole to feed the troops every meal for the next two weeks.

But suddenly there are three orders for the waiter. 'Daddy, I want a toast and Vegemite.' 'Daddy, I want Weet Bix and orange juice.' And 'Daddy, I want a googie egg with a face drawn on it, and some toast soldiers.' Already the kitchen is under stress. And, damn, the lamb is burning.

And who knows what the kids have for lunch? He's forgotten to ask. So he'll just have to ask them — trusting each in turn to describe *exactly* what Mummy normally supplies.

And so he packs the three little lunch bags. The first with a chocolate milk and a jelly crystal sandwich. The second with a Mars Bar and a mini pizza. And the third with six Roll-ups and a can of Coke.

'It's what Mummy always gives us,' they chorus, suddenly realising they are on to a very good wicket. 'And then, after she picks us up after school, it's direct to Toys For Us for the weekly buy-up.'

His eyes narrow. Could it be that someone's having a lend of him? Who could he ask that would know? Possibly the babysitter. If only he could find her number. Or, for that matter, her name. Not that it's that easy to read the phone book, what with the thick, acrid smoke that's billowing up from the stove.

Maybe it *was* too ambitious trying to cook 56 portions of Provencal Lamb Ragout, and all before school.

Still, it is great to see the kids acting as a team — passing the buckets of water up the chain to the fireman. It's the sort of early morning activity that can really bring a family together. It's been two hours since Mum left; just another 334 hours to go. If only Christopher didn't have to go to gym class with incinerated track pants.

Yet somehow this man is still full of bravado. He explains it to the fire chief: 'Efficiency, organisation, mass production, *systems*,' he proclaims. 'That's the way to run a household.' In his mind's eye he can see it all: the vacuum cleaner turbo-charged to *really* lift that dirt; the bedtime stories on a tape loop; the cot being rocked by a hand-built mechanical arm.

Yet somehow — surprise, surprise — he discovers he doesn't quite have the spare time to work on inventions. Or, indeed, to go to work at all — not now that Amy's contracted chicken pox, and Alec's come down with a rather nasty gastric, inextricably linked to his consumption of a dodgy Provencal Lamb Ragout.

But at least, in your absence, he's learning plenty of new things.

· FATHERHOOD ·

Like the fact that when a man drops his shirts on the bedroom floor they — how can we put this? — tend to stay there.

That's right. No teleporting to the washing machine. No astral travelling out to the Hills Extendaline. No unseen hand guiding them back in out of the rain. And no psychokinetic ironing, leaving them crisply starched, hanging up in rows, without any human intervention on his part.

Bummer.

Of course he'll learn to cope — especially with the aid of his neighbours, who are now queuing on the doorstep with concerned looks and armloads of casseroles: an Irish stew from Mrs Murphy, a tasty spanakopita from Mrs Sinopoulos, and a really spicy stir-fried prawn and bean-sprout dish from Mrs Lim.

Yes, it's a regular smorgasbord. And to think you said he and the kids would go hungry. That's the thing about being a man alone: he may miss out on having one woman cook for him, but instead he gets a whole streetful.

And it's even worse if you've got a helpless Mid-life Man (which brings us to Chapter Seven).

CHAPTER SEVEN

MID-LIFE MAN

or A Sudden Interest in Aphids

"Suddenly you look at him and realise that he's not the man you married. Which may leave you wondering how come you're still paying off his car."

It's your bloke's birthday. Last year you gave him a packet of flavoured condoms and a Hunters and Collectors CD. This year he's asked for some gardening gloves and a copy of *What Bird Is That?* It's on: your bloke has just entered mid-life. He's started fixating on his fading looks, is worried about his sagging virility and has become obsessed with his inadequacies at work. In severe cases he may even buy a Pajero.

But not all men are *that* desperate. Many instead will make do with a meaningless affair with a much younger woman. Take heart. Hurtful as it is, it's a lot less expensive than the Pajero.

Of course, not *all* men waste money on affairs and expensive cars. Some are too busy investing their life savings in trying to keep their own teeth and hair. And here we need to offer a word of caution: *you may think his thinning hair is cute and adorable.* Your bloke does not. Will he see the humour in the odd light-hearted bald joke? In a word: no, no, no, no, no.

The same goes for the grey hair, the weight gain, the snoring, the shot nerves and the now apparent short-term memory loss. The seventies, it seems, have taken their toll. After two decades of dabbling in mind-altering drugs, your bloke's brain cells are now disappearing faster than the South American rainforest. And although he's got perfect recall of events that occurred 25 years ago, he's now just a bit hazy on where he left the car at lunchtime.

Middle age is like that — it creeps up on a person, and suddenly it has pounced and has the bloke in its grip before he even heard the footsteps and knew to start running. Suddenly you look at him and realise that he's not the man you married. Which may leave you wondering how come you're still paying off his car.

There's only one way this wild man of rock and roll is going to pull through — he'll have to spend the next two decades in a comfy chair sipping chamomile tea, and reading the *Reader's Digest*.

And then he'll start wallowing in the nostalgia — tuning into a hits and memories station, and becoming strangely excited that his beloved Jim Morrison is now available as lift music.

As a baby boomer he's always been convinced his was the only generation to know how to live; the generation that discovered sex, drugs and rock and roll. But these days it all seems a bit difficult — he's far too tired for sex, his concerned 26-year-old doctor has advised him against drugs, and the last time he listened to live music was during *Mickey on Ice* at Westfield Shoppingtown.

Thank goodness he can still be trendy — dressed like all the other aging baby boomers in his 100 per cent Mambo surgical truss.

Whipper-Snipping Days

Yet the most frightening aspect of his mid-life crisis is when he finds himself acting like his father — taking animatedly about aphids, retouching the downpipes, and getting tense whenever Judy and Chris next door forget to whipper-snip their edges.

Somehow, mysteriously, he finds he knows the names of several flowering shrubs, and he's so committed to the dream of friable soil that when Bobo the cat passes on he seriously floats the idea of composting her.

Once he was preoccupied with sex; now it's superannuation. And just like sex, he can't get enough of it. Especially if it involves a good roll-over. And — suddenly — he's also pretty excited by the prospect of a 24-hour sale at Target, the whole issue of household pest control, and the thrilling new range of Heritage Colours. And if he paints anything else Brunswick Green frankly you'll have to leave.

Try to be sympathetic. In these weeks, months — sorry, years — your partner is coming to terms with thwarted hopes, unachieved desires, and some trying new experiences. Such as:

• Discovering the insolent youngster hanging around in the doctor's surgery is, in fact, the doctor. And worse, that he's about to give him a lecture on the care of his prostate.

• Facing the fact that his favourite T-shirt — the one bearing the legend 'Bad Attitude' — is no longer appropriate to a man who annually attends the David Jones Spring Flower Display.

• Realising he's just spent more on his new state-of-the-art lawnmower than he did on his first wife.

• Reading that Frank Zappa is dead, and that he died of natural causes.

Middle-of-the-Life Rock and Roll

Going out with much younger women, dying your hair bottle blonde, wearing absurdly inappropriate clothes and drinking far too much — all are symptoms of an acute mid-life crisis. How remarkable then that they are also the distinguishing characteristics of your average rock and roll star.

In fact, the mid-life man's favourite rock musicians — the legends of the sixties — have clearly been having a mid-life crisis since they were sixteen. Think about the sixties and suddenly it's obvious: Woodstock was not so much a three-day festival of peace, love and understanding as a very premature fortieth birthday bash.

Today, of course, the party is well and truly over — and all the real rock stars are existing on a regime of Evian water and rigorous exercise, living the lives of country squires on their baronial home-county estates. Mick Jagger is a grandfather, Ringo Starr is the much-cherished voice of Thomas the Tank Engine, and the only thing the Grateful Dead have in their joints these days is arthritis.

What's worse, these days all the old rock stars seem to look like successful accountants. And here's your bloke — who may well be a successful accountant — and all he wants is some dyed blonde hair, a 19-year-old supermodel for a girlfriend, and a CD that's just gone platinum.

As he's knotting his tie for work you can see from the faraway look in his eyes that he's lost in a very rich fantasy — that one day, some day, he could have the musicianship of Eric Clapton, the charisma of Sting, the sex appeal of Bruce Springsteen or, at very least, the liver of Keith Richards.

That's the curious thing about Australia's mental health rules: think you're Napoleon Bonaparte and you get locked up; think you're Bono from U2, and you're just another middle-aged man, home alone in front of the bedroom mirror.

What woman hasn't walked in on her man and surprised him in that most embarrassing of positions: shamelessly gratifying himself by playing a pretend guitar? There he'll be, bent double like Jimi Hendrix, letting rip a fast riff, with eyes scrunched together in sheer ecstasy — an Air Guitarist playing for his Air Audience.

Or — at the moment you walk in and spot him — he may be skidding down your polished wooden hallway on his knees, arms flailing at his Air Guitar, pelvis thrust forward, head tossed back in abandonment — just like his hero Prince, playing the hot solo from *Purple Rain*. And what a shame that — unlike Price — he's just got tangled up in Damien's tricycle. Oomph! He won't be thrusting forward *that* pelvis for a while. But still he's limping back onto his feet — and a little groin injury isn't going to stop this handsome guitar hero from satisfying his fans.

In his mind's eye he's back there on centre stage, flashing a dazzling smile into the imaginary front rows and winking at that cutie in the second row. He's hot, he's loud, and the crowd is screaming for more. Which is a coincidence, since you're screaming too. 'Turn it down, Graeme, you'll wake the baby.'

The Axeman Poseth

It's a simple fact of life: all men want to be rock stars. Prime ministers, gloomy modern novelists, prosperous plumbers, ministers of religion, middle-ranking policemen and committed scientists — all of them dream of standing with their shirts off, their torsos glistening with sweat, with 40 000 cheering fans watching every ripple in their skin-tight leather pants.

Certainly it's easy to see why most men think their chosen career doesn't quite stack up — not when it's placed against that of a professional rock hero. Whatever the virtues of a steady career with the Rural Lands Protection Board, sex-starved groupies tend to be in short supply.

And although many in the rural community appreciate the Board's sterling effort in the control of noxious weeds, rarely do you see them paying $40 and then screaming, whistling and stamping their feet, all because a Board inspector has made an appearance.

It's little wonder that men love rock and roll: it's the one place in the world where the old rules apply. Women still do the right thing: stare adoringly, applaud adoringly and listen to his words for hours at a stretch. And, best of all, there are even security guards — just in case any woman tries to interrupt. Ahhh, if only every office meeting could be like this.

Meanwhile the men can do what they do best — strutting about, showing off, and getting paid shitloads of money. Women may have their vision of a post-feminist utopia, but the men's utopia has already arrived, and it's called the Australian rock industry.

So no wonder your bloke is out there right now — practising in front of the sliding door to the porch. In the reflection he thinks he's Diesel, even if, from where you're standing, he looks more like Meat Loaf.

But look on the bright side — at least he's finally getting a bit of exercise. Creep out of the room. Pretend you didn't notice. With the help of Air Guitar, he might even work off some of that paunch.

THE AIR GUITAR SONGBOOK

You've noticed that your husband is playing Air Guitar, but you don't have the foggiest which famous rock song he thinks he is playing. Why not check out the patented *Air Guitar Songbook* — the world's only songbook without a single musical note?

Your bloke may even like to try out some of these new tunes, with these simple note-by-note instructions — all, of course, in the privacy of his own million-seater mind.

Smoke on the Water (Deep Purple)
Grimace. Grimace. Pelvic thrust. Pelvic thrust.
Lean back. Strum.

Heart of Gold (Neil Young)
Soulful look. Soulful look. Rhythmic sway. Strum.

Born in the USA (Bruce Springsteen)
Strum, strike meaningful pose. Flex pecs. Strum.

Sweet Child o' Mine (Guns n' Roses)
Both hands in front of crotch. Move fingers rapidly.
Squint. Tilt back head.

Rockin' All Over the World (Status Quo)
Plant feet very far apart. Bend over. Wave hair.
Wave hair.

My Generation (The Who)
Hold left arm out. Swing right arm in circular motion. Repeat. Kick imaginary speakers.

Purple Haze (Jimi Hendrix)
Lean back. Bite left forearm as if it were guitar
neck. Set fire to bin.

Tubular Bells (Mike Oldfield)
Stand very still for 40 minutes.

Or, if he finds Air Guitar too challenging, he may prefer to make a selection from *The Air Microphone Songbook*:

Too Much in Love (Jimmy Barnes)
Squint, clutch Air Microphone, shriek, thrust arm
around imaginary bass guitarist, shriek.

When a Man Loves a Woman (Michael Bolton)
Clutch Air Microphone, soulful look, soulful look,
flick appalling hair, emote, emote, flick appalling
hair, emote.

• THE JOY OF BLOKES •

The Even Older Bloke

How will you know when your bloke has moved on from his mid-life crisis, and into the next fulfilling phase, the twilight years? It's easy: just examine his trouser belt.

Just as a woman's hemline descends to a sensible length in her more mature years, so with advancing years does the top of a man's pants drift ever skyward. In fact, his pants keep riding up until they find a new home hitched halfway up his chest, lodged on a comfortable little ledge right under the nipple.

More remarkable still, anthropologists report the phenomenon is cross-cultural — whether it's a lap-lap, a sarong or a pair of ancient lederhosen the older gentleman's apparel always defies the laws of gravity.

Other warning signs are that he demands his own chair, compulsively listens to the TV and radio news and goes into a complete decline if he doesn't get his lunch by 11.45 am. Of course, older men have been like this for generations; what's exciting about watching the aging baby boomer is discovering exactly how high a pair of Levi's 501s can drift.

Which brings us, with suspicious neatness, to the topic of men and clothes.

CHAPTER EIGHT

SHOPPING FOR CLOTHES

or The Quick Way to End a Marriage

"Peril stalks with every new dress. Indeed, just as marriages mostly begin with the question, 'Do you take this woman to be your lawful wedded wife?' so they usually end with the phrase, 'So what do I look like in this dress?'"

SHOPPING ALONE

Man as Victim

In day to day life your bloke puts on a pretty good show of being a competent achiever, a fearless decision maker, a man in control of his own destiny. But then the black day comes when the bum has finally gone in his going-out pants, and there's one too many ink stains on the pocket of his drip-dry shirt. He can put it off no longer. He has to go shopping.

And that means he has finally to confront his greatest fear — coming face to face with a snappily dressed young salesman, alone in a flimsy change-room, armed with nothing but a battered Bankcard and his own dwindling self-esteem.

No wonder he's scared as he walks into the maelstrom they call Leisure Wear. Through the gaps in the change-room curtains he can already see the atrocities being committed on the other customers — all of them meek, taste-impaired males being led to a fashion slaughter.

There's the muscle-bound apprentice mechanic who's just popped in for a new pair of khaki King Gees — but is currently being forced by the perky young salesman into a $70 blouson shirt and a pair of smudged-apricot drawstring pants.

Or, next booth along, there's Barry, the outer suburban police sergeant who, due to a wildly misplaced confidence in the advice of his salesman, looks likely to attend his own sixtieth birthday dinner dressed in a parachute-silk jumpsuit and a 'fun' bow-tie.

Or, perhaps most disturbing of all, there's the silver-haired Supreme Court Judge just now emerging from the last cubicle wearing some enormous surf-grunge board shorts and a Stussy baseball cap worn the wrong way round.

After witnessing these tragedies, your bloke will do anything to avoid being trapped by this salesman, which is why he's trying to sneak through the racks in Day Wear, trying to sidestep any pressure, when — *oops!* — he runs head-on into Ashley, the smartly dressed 21-year-old salesman.

And with one glimpse of that breezy smile, he can tell Ashley's working on commission. The game is up.

Fitting Him Up

Your bloke may as well throw down his Bankcard, put his hands in the air, and invite Ashley to take a chest measurement. They stare each other down. Ashley is immaculate; in his taupe soft-wash double-pleated trousers and zip-front dress shirt with button-down collar, he is a picture straight from the pages of his own catalogue. And with one glance into Ashley's implacable eyes, your bloke can tell exactly what the young salesman is thinking.

'Sir *has* rather let himself go.'

Within five minutes, your man has joined the other male victims — the cop, the judge and the mechanic — in the change-rooms, semi-naked and shivering in his red Rio undies and black socks, about to spend 45 minutes of torture dutifully trying on Ashley's high-fashion selection.

And as he emerges from the booth into the full glare of the crowded shop, squeezed into a pair of caramel crushed linen Gatsby shorts, teamed with a brushed cotton Matelot shirt in navy and white, a cream cravat and navy espadrilles, all set off by a courageous suede cap, he ponders whether Ashley had a particularly unhappy childhood.

The crowd of shoppers stops and stares. And suddenly your bloke knows what people mean when they talk about non-chemical castration. He's dressed to kill — and Ashley's the one he wants to murder.

'Oh, yes. Very smart, sir,' beams Ashley, signalling to the other salesman to stop sniggering.

'But,' your bloke stammers, 'don't you think the cap is a bit much?'

Ashley bridles and draws himself up to his full metre and a half. 'But, sir, it's a fashion statement.' Yes. The type that can be taken down and used in evidence against you.

By now Ashley is circling for the kill. 'It's a versatile outfit,' he enthuses. 'You can dress it up. Or you can dress it down. And the fit is perfect on Sir.'

Your bloke *wants* to say no, but something is stopping him. Maybe it's the rather enthusiastic way Ashley's knotted the cream cravat.

'I don't know if I'm really ready for this sort of gear,' your guy splutters. 'Maybe I need to have a think.'

'But, Sir,' insists Ashley. 'This is the last one in your size. And it's so ... today. Isn't it, Anthony?'

Anthony approaches. Oh no. Reinforcements. Your bloke knows when he's beaten. It's all over. He removes the cream silk cravat and waves it above his head in surrender. He feels ridiculous, he looks ridiculous, and he just wants to go home and burn the clothes. Just as soon as he's signed over a month's salary for this travesty.

And when he gets home, please be gentle with this emotionally shipwrecked sailor boy. Remember, you can always make him take it back. Back to:

• THE JOY OF BLOKES •

The Returns Counter

The Dark Underbelly of Modern Retailing

If your bloke was daunted by the experience of buying his hideous ensemble, just wait until he tries to take it back. Whatever his drawbacks, Ashley had seemed such a friendly, personable young man last Saturday morning. Come Monday, Ashley's become an embittered veteran of the war that is leisure wear.

And he's treating your bloke as if he'd just ripped the lieutenant's stripes off his sleeves, which in a way he has. By bringing back his purchase, poor Ashley's just lost his commission.

Suddenly it's Dr Jekyll and Mr Hyde. 'Returning it?' Ashley grimaces through lips of string, staring your bloke boldly in the eye. 'Why?'

No way is your bloke going to tell Ashley the truth: that he's returning it because *you* told him he had to. And so he flounders. He claims he doesn't like the cut. He claims he doesn't care for the colour. Anything to get out of revealing that his six-year-old son said the scarf made him look like 'a big girl'.

Ashley bridles and looks at his watch. After having drowned your bloke in attention on Saturday, Ashley now curtly announces that he's unable to discuss the matter any further. It's time for his break. And so he passes your bloke on to Anthony.

What a shame that Anthony will be busy for some considerable time dealing with a scarlet-faced Supreme Court Judge attempting to return a pair of surf-grunge shorts. The judge has a good grounding in consumer advocacy and he's not getting an inch out of Anthony.

Knowing that he's beaten your bloke returns home, to place the sad little package at the back of the wardrobe, waiting for the time, in a year or maybe two, that you'll pack the lot into the bag for the Salvos.

And next time you see a Queensland flood victim on the telly kitted out like a French matelot with a jaunty suede cap, you'll know that somehow it's all been for the best.

SHOPPING TOGETHER

— and its Role in Marriage

Meltdown

The alternative to these disasters is to go shopping together so that you can gently assist your partner to choose an outfit that won't scare the local kiddies. And the trick is never to let your man think you are trying to control his choices. He needs to feel as if he's in command — even when he's putty in your manipulative hands.

Certainly, men can choose between many methods of dressing appallingly. Older men may have got the impression that they should dress like Johnny Depp. Men the age of Johnny Depp may accidentally decide to dress like Johnny Howard. And most disturbing of all, John Howard types may decide to throw off the Pringle cardigan and grey pants and dare to be different.

They all should be discouraged — but in the gentlest and most diplomatic ways. When he plucks the offending item from the rack, try not to let loose a cat call or holler 'Don't barf me out, mister'. Better by far to use one of the sure-fire phrases perfected by women throughout history. Phrases like:

> 'It's nice — except for the funny way it rides around your crotch.'

> 'Great — but can the buttons handle that much strain?'

'That's great — and it makes you look *just* like your father.'

'Not bad — I saw one just like it in the Mardi Gras.'

'Terrific — but are you sure they're not meant for girls?'

and

'You know you're going to have to breathe out sometime, Gregory.'

But you'll also need positive reinforcement when he finally chances upon something that you like. On no account be enthusiastic and say you think he looks really sexy in it. Tell him the *17-year-old salesgirl* thinks he looks really sexy in it. You'll never see a garment go faster under the barcode scanner. Well done! Mission accomplished!

Now it's your turn to go shopping, with your man tagging along. By and large, most blokes would rather submit to a three-day tax audit than help their partner choose a new dress. They know the truth: there is no faster and more final way to end a relationship.

Peril stalks with every new dress. Indeed, just as marriages mostly begin with the question, 'Do you take this woman to be your lawful wedded wife?' so they usually end with the phrase, 'So what do I look like in this dress?'

Suddenly your bloke is struck dumb. Not since Bill Clinton tried to avoid answering all those questions about Whitewater has a man engaged in so much shifty evasion. He knows he can't win.

He can say you look gorgeous, and suffer the consequences when, $180 dollars later, you get home and realise it's all been a terrible mistake.

Or he can tell the truth right there and then, admit the cut is unflattering and it makes you look, how can he put it — *stout* — and see

• SHOPPING FOR CLOTHES •

his marriage end on the spot.

And it is *soooo* easy to end it. Especially considering the sort of phrases which nervous men have uttered — to their eternal regret — outside the change-room doors throughout time.

The Family Wreckers
— or Things Your Bloke Should Never,
Ever say Outside the Change-room Doors

'Darling, it makes you look a bit ... ummm ... matronly.'

'I don't know ... hasn't your mum got one of those?'

'Those horizontal stripes are just a bit ... er ... prominent across the beam.'

'Wouldn't you feel more comfortable if it was ... um ... a couple of sizes bigger?'

'Are you sure it isn't meant for a younger woman?'

(*confused*) 'Exactly what effect were you aiming at, dear?'

and

'I think it's nice, but maybe a bit ... er ... optimistic.'

And on it goes until you've tried on ten dresses, and are ready to ask the killer question: 'Darling, which do you think looked best on me?' And it's then you can see the real panic registering in his eyes.

Of course it's a trick question: there is no right answer. But like a man climbing the scaffold he is determined to be brave to the last. He plucks out a number: 'The first one.' He flinches, and readies himself for your standard reply: 'Oh? And you are saying the other nine made me look fat?'

For most men this signals a sudden need to window-shop for fertiliser. But there are some blokes who won't chicken out. There are blokes who will stay there with you, right there in the store — ignoring you while they leaf through the latest bra catalogue.

And when you emerge from the change room, defeated and dejected, you'll discover these blokes enjoying a sparkling conversation with Melissa, the nubile — and size 10 — sales assistant.

'It's useless,' you'll tell your bloke. 'There's nothing here that really suits me.'

And it's then, in all innocence, that he'll make the fatal mistake of trying to be helpful. 'Why don't you try on the dress that Melissa's wearing. *She* looks stunning.'

Oh, yes. It's time to go home.

CHAPTER NINE

THE DECLINE OF MAN

Blokes at Their Worst

"Panadol? Aspro? Sudafed? He looks at you incredulously. *They're* for girls. Even to suggest them proves that you haven't grasped QUITE HOW SICK HE IS."

PART ONE
COMPETITIVE MAN

There are many things that women find surprising about men. And one of them is this: that within even the most spongy-bottomed of the species there lingers sufficient aggression to launch World War III.

Consider, for example, what happens when a man misses the ball in a friendly game of squash. Does he maturely take note of his error? Does he quietly work on improving his next shot? Not quite.

Instead he throws his racquet to the ground and lets loose a scream of such bloodcurdling intensity that you'd think that at the very least someone has just chopped off his penis. Which in a sense they have.

Even the most effete man believes his manhood is at stake when he's placed in a competitive situation. That's why they overturn the Squatter board in a blind rage, just because their five year old was first to irrigate his paddocks. And that's why your bloke lies awake at night, sweating mad over the bastard boss and how he's been passed over for promotion — and wondering whether a conviction for first-degree murder might affect his superannuation entitlements.

Why *are* men so competitive? Scientists believe that much masculine behaviour may result from the way the male brain is regularly bathed in a naturally occurring liquid known as 'beer'. And this beer means men will compete over anything — in particular the amount of beer they can ingest during a given period.

What would happen if men could give birth? Naturally, they'd turn it into a competition: 'You should have seen the bloke in the next labour ward,' they'd say, as they showed their mates their birth video on action replay. 'He was struggling and straining, and out pops this little five-pounder. What a poofter! Mate, mine was a 12-pounder with a 20-hour labour, and we bonded right on touchdown. As for the breast feeding — it was up with the footy jersey and the little tiger was away.'

But luckily men do not need to compete with each other over birth. They've got a million other things to compete over. And none quite as absurd as the competition over how hot a curry they can consume — as you will discover at Sanjay's Hot Indian Curry House.

Meet the Curry Kings

Here they all are, your bloke and his mates, in the privacy of a bustling Asian curry house, and — within minutes of sitting down — the jostling to be head stag has begun.

'I love curries,' says Dave. 'And the hotter, the better,' says your bloke. 'Oh, I've had some curries in my time,' crows Mikey, 'curries that would burn your socks off.'

'Yeah,' says Dave, 'but I bet you haven't eaten dog curry — it was *beeeewdiful*.'

Your bloke bristles, and thinks of poor Sargey-Boy's hindquarters. But that doesn't stop him throwing himself into the orgy of big-noting competition. 'Well, dog's all right if you like your curries mild,' he boasts, 'but it's nothing on the chilli monkey brains that Gazza and I had in Macau. Then you're talking *hot*.'

And on it goes. On and on. The relentless sounds of blokes showing off. You and the other women at the table sigh, and place a modest order for a mild chicken curry.

It's going to be a long night: your food arrives, and the men are still arguing about what *they* are going to order. Dave is still in overseas mode — reliving his culinary tour of Penang, chilli by excruciating chilli. Only one thing stops him, and that's the waiter, Sanjay, approaching to take their order.

'How would you like your curry, sir — mild, medium or hot?' The men reply, as one: 'As hot as buggery, thanks mate.'

Sanjay looks at them enigmatically. Several centuries of Western colonialism, and finally he has the chance of revenge. The ghost of a smile passes across his face, and he turns toward the kitchen: 'Just as you like, sirs.'

Back at the table, the conversation has drifted to the topic of do-it-yourself home improvements. Dave's just built a verandah. Hardwood uprights, tallowwood slats, galvanised bullet-head nails. 'Beeeewdiful, mate.' But naturally your bloke has built a bigger verandah.

The women stare at their plates. They can't believe it. It's *soooo* embarrassing. Out on the town for a sophisticated evening, and all their blokes can do is sit around and compare the size of their decks.

Sanjay brings in the first course — some prawn balls. The men wolf them down. Inside the pastry it's almost solid chilli. This is not a prawn ball, it's an incendiary device. It's like munching on a flaming barbecue starter.

All five men have tears streaming down their cheeks, and several appear to be having trouble breathing. Finally Dave manages to wipe away the tears and make clear his feelings to the waiting Sanjay. '*Beeeewdiful, mate.*'

'Yeah,' your bloke agrees, 'it wasn't at all bad — especially if you like your prawn balls mild. Myself, I prefer them hot.'

'Yeah, next time make it hot,' chant the men, as they chug-a-lug the Riesling.

'Yes, sir,' replies Sanjay impassively, with a small click of his heels. He had intended to avenge the colonial past of his own nation, but instead, here's the chance to avenge the treatment of the whole Asian sub-continent. He returns to the kitchen. This is war.

Back at the table, the men are trying to disguise the fact that they have virtually lost the power of speech. Their taste buds are screaming in pain, and seem unlikely to ever function properly again. Not that this is going to stop them showing off about the wine which each man has brought in his Decor two-bottle soft cooler. Still blinded by tears they all reach for a glass of their own offerings, in order to prove that, although they might feel a bit dizzy, they still know a good drop.

'Beeeewdiful cabernet merlot I brought,' brags your bloke, his eyes still streaming, as he accidentally swigs down a small bowl of soy sauce. 'It really seems to go with this Asian food.'

'Yeah, very typical of the district,' agrees the oblivious Dave, as he downs the finger bowl and chokes on the slice of lemon. 'And quite a fruity aftertaste.'

Sanjay slips back to the table, dutifully serving the lamb curry. 'Oh, I do hope our humble establishment has managed to accommodate your most sophisticated palates,' says Sanjay, unable to stop the smirk creeping on to his face.

'No worries, buddy,' beams your bloke, sweating profusely. 'You know, we've all been to Asia.'

'Yeah, I've had monkey brains in Macau,' boasts Dave, swinging his arm around Sanjay's shoulder in a misplaced gesture of friendship.

The women sink deeper into their chairs. If only the blokes would get back to comparing the size of their decks.

Suddenly you notice that groups of Sanjay's relatives are peering eagerly around the kitchen door. Other groups of the local Malaysian community have been alerted, and are being bused in. They haven't felt this exhilarated since they got rid of the British in 1957.

The blokes spoon into the lamb curry. This dish wasn't made over a stove, it was made in a smelter. They dip in the spoon and it turns red and bends. In the searing desert of their own minds, even these men are starting to have their doubts.

Why are the six chefs peering around the kitchen door, poking each other in the ribs and sniggering? Why has Sanjay's ancient grandmother been carried down from upstairs in her dressing gown and why is she now training her opera glasses on the group of diners?

And why is there a phalanx of people from the Malaysian community gathered outside, peering through the restaurant's front window and humming national songs?

It's Dave that speaks, a touch of nervousness tugging at what's left of his vocal chords. 'Um, mate — why don't you go first?'

Gingerly your bloke takes a modest serving and places a single piece of lamb into his mouth. First he turns white, then mauve, then a disturbing shade of crimson. His gall-bladder has just burst into flames, and his manhood is on the line. Finally he speaks.

'*Beeeewdiful*,' he stutters, fainting forward into his mixed vegetables.

Sanjay rushes to his side, a concerned look on his face. 'Can I get you anything, sir?'

'Don't worry about him, mate,' says Dave. 'He's just disappointed. He was hoping for a hot one.'

PART TWO: MAN AT HIS *VERY* WORST

But showing off about curries is so stupid that, let's face it, it becomes just a little endearing. It is not a man at his *very* worst. But that day will surely come.

It will be an ordinary day and you'll come home from work, fling open your bedroom door, and find a crazed felon in your bed. He'll be wearing a full black woollen balaclava, out of which will stare two crazy feverish eyes, and he'll be moaning and writhing as if he's just received a shotgun blast to the stomach.

It is, of course, your partner. And, yes, he has the flu.

'I'm very, very sick,' he chokes, his voice muffled by the balaclava, 'and I'm trying to sweat it out.'

Women of Australia, face facts: nobody gets sicker than blokes. And that's why they tend to favour the most peculiar and mediaeval of cures. Their policy is 'Anything, as long as it's attention-getting'.

Sweating it out. Taking cold showers. Lying prone on the bathroom floor. Having their backs beaten to 'loosen the chest'. Eating raw garlic. In fact, they're only a poultice away from ordering a sacrificial pig's bladder and 500 grams of live leeches.

Panadol? Aspro? Sudafed? He looks at you incredulously. *They're for girls.* Even to suggest them proves that you haven't grasped QUITE HOW SICK HE IS.

He is suffering, ohhhhhh, how he is suffering. And you've got to admit he seems a little warm. In fact, he's lying in a pool of sweat, with a throbbing red face and a temperature that is pushing 47 degrees.

A doctor would react by pronouncing him clinically dead. *You* react by switching off the electric blanket, removing two of the doonas, and insisting that the balaclava gets the heave-ho. Apart from anything else, it's traumatising the dog.

'It's no normal flu,' he wheezes. 'This one's a real mongrel.'

Of course it's a mongrel. No man has ever caught a normal flu, a regular, Joe-average, garden-variety flu. When have you ever heard a man explaining: 'Don't worry — it's just a tickle in the throat.' Oh, no, not them. One cough and it's the Deadly Beijing Mongrel Killer Flu.

And most disturbing of all is the speed with which your bloke contracted this disease. No matter what the virus, his incubation period is always the same: exactly five minutes after you've announced that *you* are feeling ill. He'd love to be sympathetic — and to wait on you hand and foot for the next few days — but, alas, that's no longer possible. Anyone can see that, compared to you, he's contracted a far worse case.

It's the same every time you contract anything — even cystitis. He's always got it worse. Especially if you've left a medical dictionary anywhere near his side of the bed. Within minutes he'll be flipping through and the complications will be setting in — the TB, the leprosy, the dengue fever. He hasn't got a chance.

In a frail, broken voice he'll ask you whether you think he'll survive. And you'll have to be gentle as you break the news — there's a slim chance he'll pull through. Of course, he's unconvinced. Perhaps he'll make it, but only if you do your bit. And for that you'll need the patience of a saint, the chicken soup recipes of a country mum, and the strength-inspiring bosoms of a *Carry On* nurse.

He also seems to have regressed to childhood, and is only really content if you speak to him in baby talk — plumping his pillows and telling him he's being a 'bwave wittle soldier'. He'll smile wanly, looking up from his Bed of Pain. 'Perhaps tomorrow you could bring me a little prezzie from the shops,' he'll say, before asking if you'd mind switching on *Alvin and the Chipmunks*.

And through it all you'll watch astounded as he gives his Logie-winning performance — the wan looks, the slight tremble in the hand, the involuntary shiver when he gets up, the stumbling gait, and his speciality, The Courageous Little Smile That Masks Indescribable Pain. Anything to get you to give him just a little more sympathy.

And all this for a head cold. When he actually gets the flu it'll be the death scene from *Camille*.

Yet there are times when the attention-seeking stops; times when he'll be creeping up the hallway, hoping you don't notice. And that's when he tiptoes into the kitchen in order to keep his 'liquids up' — bloke-talk for yet another medicinal glass of the Wynns Hermitage.

Don't try and warn him off it. Sure, it may be a medical fact that no one gets sicker than men — but no bloke is ever *quite* sick enough to go off the grog.

CHAPTER TEN

SUDDENLY SINGLE

or Meeting Mr Possibly Right

"One can always tell if two Australian workers are having an affair, as they're the only two people in the office actually getting on with their work."

Swans always mate for life, but human beings haven't got such a good record. With the best will in the world some relationships hit the wall, and the time comes to divide the cutlery, split the bills, and argue over who gets to keep the Elton John CDs. ('You keep them'; 'No, really, I insist, they're *yours*.')

What causes the break up? It may be that some of his little habits have finally got on your nerves. The way he clips his toenails. The way he chews gum in bed. And the way he sneaked off to Hamilton Island last week with a 20-year-old aerobics instructor called Juanita.

Whatever the cause, breaking up is still emotionally tough, and you'll struggle to overcome your guilt and disappointment. But at least his pain will be worse — especially in the lower back after ten days with the pneumatic Juanita.

Psychotherapists have determined that women pass through three stages of grieving after the death of a relationship. These are:

1. Disbelief
2. Sorrow, and
3. The radical new haircut.

It is a statistical fact that the Australian hairdressing industry largely survives on the giddy turbulence of human relationships. But sooner or later the pain will pass. And with any luck your hair may even grow back. Suddenly you'll realise that life as a freewheeling woman can be fun: that there are holidays to have, people to see, careers to pursue and — in the shorter term — wigs to rent.

This is the upside of being suddenly single. For the first time in ages you're wearing the clothes *you* like, going to the places *you* want, and spending time with the people *you* prefer. Your life has become compromise-free. At last you can rent *Enchanted April* for the tenth time without seeing your bloke looking aggrieved, standing glumly in the video store fingering a copy of *Cliffhanger*.

That's the point: if the mood takes you — and chances are it will — you'll be free to spend the whole weekend on your own, dressed in your tracky dacks and dorky sweater, eating Hoboken Crunch ice cream by the tub and weepin' into your ole Willy Nelson CDs. Ahhh, ain't life grand.

Yet the day will surely come when you'll surprise yourself with thoughts of love, or — let's be brutally honest — lust. Suddenly you'll have thoughts of leaping back into the uncertain world that is dating. *Off* comes the dorky sweater. *Off* come the daggy tracky pants. *Off* come the Willy Nelson CDs. And *on* go the Lycra running shorts. Now is the moment to start shedding your lethargy and pain; and, more's the point, to start shedding those three months of Hoboken Crunch ice cream.

Yet just when you are about to kick-start your love life, your mind will be tormented by questions. Questions like:

- Are men really worth it?

- Have you got the energy for dating and its self-conscious small-talk? and
---
- Wouldn't you be better to do something more emotionally satisfying with your Saturday nights, like spending them home alone in front of *The Bill*.

Everyone goes through this period of doubt, but sooner or later you'll be forced to change. For a start, *The Bill* will go into January recess. And a whole summer season of *Birds of a Feather* would be enough to force anyone out of the house.

Throughout it all your shacked-up girlfriends will be encouraging you to play the field as, one after another, they whisper into your ear: 'Take heart, mate, there's plenty more fish in the sea.' And you can't deny they're right — it's just that, oddly enough, you're after a man.

Where can you find one? On the big bright merry-go-round of love, that's where.

The Merry-Go-Round of Love

How is the modern woman supposed to find a good man? Or to put the question another way: there may well be 8.4 million men in Australia, but where are they all on a Saturday night?

Certainly you'll need to show some discernment in your choice of venue, and avoid picking up your new man somewhere unsuitable — such as in the lobby of the Family Court. Take note, the Court has a perfectly good coffee shop for just that purpose.

The Joy of Blokes, after lengthy opinion surveys, also cannot recommend meeting Mr Possibly Right by either a) answering obscene phone calls with the phrase 'tell me more'; or b) making small-talk during the police line up.

Far better, on the available evidence, are the more traditional methods, such as meeting your new bloke at work. That way, you can have all the fun of trying to keep your affair secret from the rest of your workmates — while enjoying the intrigue of never chatting or laughing together during work hours. (It's interesting to note that one can always tell if two Australian workers are having an affair, as they're the only two people in the office actually getting on with their work.)

Of course, the one problem with the work environment is that it can be hard to tell if someone's interested in romance. But, as the advice columnists say, only a coward would let her insecurities get the better of her. You've got to take control, be courageous and Own Your Own Destiny.

If there's a real electricity between you and a man at work, you should do what all the advice manuals suggest — walk boldly over to his desk and say the words that will change your life for ever: 'Jamie, I love you, I've always loved you, and I can tell you feel for me too.'

And that's when Jamie may well look up and meet your gaze: 'Well, that's very flattering,' he'll stammer, 'and I'd love to be really good friends, but I must say I've never thought of you in quite that way, Jenny.'

At this time, you might find yourself painfully stuck for words. But you could start by pointing out that your name's not Jenny.

It is humiliations such as these which have encouraged some women to try more radical methods — such as going on swinging holidays to Bali. These are advertised regularly for the under thirties — it's just a shame you didn't realise they were talking IQ points.

As an alternative you could try what Helen Gurley Brown cunningly suggested in her book *Sex and the Single Girl*, and try doing a course — especially one in which female students are in short supply. Back in 1970, Ms Gurley Brown recommended courses for car mechanics and panel beaters. In the mid-nineties, *The Joy of Blokes* goes one further and suggests you sign up for the official training program to become a Jesuit priest. There you'll find men galore. And what do you know? — not one is married.

If you're really desperate, however, you might be better to go on a blind date — otherwise known as the Russian Roulette of Romance. Your friends might tell you this guy is handsome, intelligent and a man of real convictions, and, indeed, the police fraud computer may

> ## WORLD'S FIVE WORST EVER PICK-UP LINES
>
> 1. No really, I *love* chubby girls.
>
> 2. Help me out will you, I'm going for a record.
>
> 3. How about it, babe? There's only twelve hours before my condoms expire.
>
> 4. But tonight's our big chance — my wife's out all night, giving birth.
>
> 5. Has anyone told you that you look just like Demi Moore, only fatter?

well reveal seven or eight.

Other women have had success going back through their old address books: that former boyfriend you so thoughtlessly cast off in 1985 may well be worth a second look. After all, your standards may have been higher in the eighties. Back then you demanded a partner who was caring, sensitive and clean; these days, you'd settle for clean.

But when you've tried everything else there's still the newspaper singles' column — that glorious utopia in which every inhabitant is unattached, sensitive, financially secure and absolutely obsessed with bushwalking.

But if you want to succeed, the modern woman has to learn some translation skills.

Singles Columns:
What they say and what they mean

'Mr 35'	...	He's pushing 50
'Enjoys fine wine'	...	Alcoholic
'Pythonesque sense of humour'	...	Crashing bore
'Loves fine food'	...	Porker
'Loves hang gliding'	...	Liar
'Incurable romantic'	...	Sex addict
'Has wide tastes'	...	Pervert
'Seeks to break out of the hum-drum of daily life'	...	Adulterer
'Enjoys spirited debates'	...	Intellectual bully
'Loves feminine women'	...	Misogynist patriarch
'Loves vintage wine and art-house movies'	...	Wanker
'Well-travelled professional man'	...	Drug-runner
'Financially secure'	...	Mean with money
'Seeks ongoing relationship'	...	Seeks cheap sex
'Seeks relationship of mutual respect'	...	Seeks cheap sex
'Seeks fun life together'	...	Seeks cheap, kinky sex

So, meeting people through the singles' column has its drawbacks. But then so does the numero uno method of meeting men — stand by folks for a chilling phrase — that's right, we're talking about *chatting up someone at a party*.

• SUDDENLY SINGLE •

Party Games

Socialising is bad enough when you're an adolescent, crammed into a kitchen crowded with awkward, socially inept and painfully shy 16 year olds; but it's that much worse twenty years later, when you find yourself crammed into a kitchen full of awkward, socially inept and just plain painful 36 year olds.

In some societies, in order to win the right to mate, one has first to endure an intricate and solemn ritual of initiation. In Australia, we are forced to eat Jatz and warmed cubed cheese.

Everyone knows the scene: an entirely empty lounge room, the Red Hot Chilli Peppers at full belt, and one tanked-up party-goer unconscious on the couch, while up the hallway the kitchen looks like the Tokyo subway at peak hour — a solid mass of hormone-drenched humanity, squeezed into a fluoro-lit kitchenette and fuelled with a mixture of hope, desire and all-too-sweet riesling. And each time the host opens the fridge, the whole room has to breathe in.

We've all been here before, and more often than not returned home with nothing more lasting than a bad headache. But hope is the most resilient part of the human heart, and some tiny, absurdly optimistic voice can always be heard in the back of the mind of every single party-goer, shouting: 'Stick around, mingle, this is the party where you could finally meet h*im*.'

And so, reluctantly, you take another swig of warm reisling and cram yourself tighter into the corner, with the deep freeze cutting into your back and an unpleasant view of a cigarette butt drowning in some sad taramasalata, as you try to suss out the smooth-talking man who's just sidled up to you.

And somehow you just know, from the optimistic look on his face, that here is a man with a mission; a man who is wearing his lucky undies.

So you relax and listen to his conversation — and wonder whether he is saying exactly what he means. Let's fact it, this guy is not talking English, he's conversing in Party-speak, and you're going to need a translation:

> *He says:* I'm very concerned about ozone depletion.
> *He means:* I'm single, I'm available, and I'm interested.

> *He says:* It's refreshing to meet a woman who cares about lead levels.
> *He means:* It's refreshing to meet a woman who wears such tight clothes.

> *He says:* Actually, I'm a feminist, myself — I've just read Susan Faludi.
> *He means:* In that dress, your breasts are really quite staggering.

And, then, towards the end of the night:

> *He says:* What a shame you've got to go.
> *He means:* Quick! Quick! Only an hour left to crack on to somebody else.

Will *you* survive the dating game? Only if you choose the man that's right for you. Which brings us to Chapter Eleven.

CHAPTER ELEVEN

MAN: THE MENU

Select from Our Extensive List

"When you were dating, Brad used to laugh at your father and call him that 'mad old bastard'. Now only close relatives can tell them apart."

For every woman, there's a perfect man. It's just that yours may well have lived in Iceland in the fifth century. So what's on offer in the here and now?

Run your eyes over this lot and count up how many *you've* experienced.

The Prince

Since you've moved in with Neil you've spent months encouraging him to do his share of the housework — and finally you've ended up with this sweet, cooperative bloke who's the envy of all your friends. And then in one single, ghastly afternoon all your hard work goes out the window. He announces that you're going home to Sunday lunch with his mum.

And it's then, as you walk into the family home, that it hits you: unwittingly you've shacked up with royalty. From the way his mother is treating him, your bloke is actually Crown Prince Neil, the heir to all he surveys — the TV remote, the video, the beer fridge, the booze cabinet.

As soon as he arrives, HRH simply plonks himself into his Jason Recliner throne, kicks off his runners, and demands a beer be brought forth. And his court obeys, with frenzied excitement.

His mother urges the Monarch to not lift a single royal finger. As you watch aghast, squads of sisters are dispatched to make the humble offerings: 'Perhaps a beer nut, Neil?' 'Would you like a Jatz and cabanossi?' 'If you prefer, Nana could jog down to the shops for some dolmades.'

To your horror, a smile of satisfaction creeps across your bloke's face and he lets loose a contented sigh. 'Oh Nana — that would be lovely, I just love dolmades.' And off she goes, lacing up her Nike joggers over her support stockings, and giving a little bow as she backs through the door.

Months of training and it's all gone out the window.

Suddenly you twig the royal visit has been planned for weeks — and by command of His Majesty, Mum has cooked his favourite: a roast with all the trimmings. You can't believe the grovelling and the fawning. And that's before Nana stumbles in, purple-faced and confused, grabbing a couple of angina tablets before handing over the dolmades. Has she collapsed, or is she merely prostrating herself before the heir apparent?

How interesting, though, that his mother seems so keen not to usurp your role — suggesting *you* might like to fetch him the sports section and a moist towelette to wipe his brow. And you'll know exactly where to stick the sports section, just as soon as you get him home.

Which is also when you can remind Prince Neil exactly what happened to the Russian Royal Family.

The Replicate

When you were dating, Brad used to laugh at your father and call him that 'mad old bastard'. Now only close relatives can tell them apart. It's spooky. Put your father in a pair of Mambo board shorts and give him a cool haircut and there you are — face to face with your new husband.

How did you do it? In a country of 18 million people you managed to find him, the only guy who makes that same disgusting sound when he eats salami. Your mother warned you about many things, but not this. For eighteen years you endured your father's tuneless shower singing, only to discover he's now passed on the sheet music.

In their novelty aprons, and standing side by side behind the kettle barbie with stubbies of cold VB in their hands, your bloke and your father are like a matching set of book-ends.

It's like you've just time-travelled into your own future, and it's scarier than anything in Nostradamus. This is a tag team effort to drive you crazy — two men who talk through movies, who both whinge about the phone bill and who both share a frenzied obsession for finding the best price for petrol. Does one woman really deserve them both?

The Great Pretender

This bloke is living in a fantasy world. In the wide open spaces of his mind he's a feminist hero. He'll tell you he once bought Naomi Wolf's *The Beauty Myth* as a sign of his solidarity; his best mate will tell you it was a cheap device to score a more intelligent style of girlfriend.

And it worked with you. All until that black moment when he accidentally referred to Ms Wolfe as 'that feminist — you know, the pretty one'.

Still, he's all for the cause. And when you have a dinner party, he'll be happy to entertain the guests with a lecture on the patriarchy — just to give you time to scrub the potatoes, slaughter the chook and do a preliminary wash-up.

He's convinced he does his half. And when you express your doubts, he's genuinely hurt. 'I do the vacuuming, *all the time*. I do the ironing, *all the time*. I clean the toilet, *all the time*.' Such is the power of his delusions, that the phrase 'all the time' actually seems to refer to one hectic afternoon in late July 1993. Like many unique events in world history, it's been celebrated ever since.

In his work life, he's always ready to prove himself a doer. And at home he's just as busy — working flat out to make sure you never, ever ask him to do his share again. And it's quite a performance. Doing the ironing he burns through your work uniform. Washing the clothes he floods the laundry. And making the kids' lunches takes him a full hour as he constantly interrupts with his questions: 'Where's the cling wrap?' 'Where's the bread?' 'Where's the ham?' And most revealing of all, 'Where's the kitchen?'

The Mad Rooter

The Mad Rooter is led through life by his penis — always beckoning him forward, like a water diviner's stick. He'll follow it anywhere — working his way through all your close acquaintances, the office and out into much of the CBD.

In his eyes life is a paddock and it's always spring. It's not that he doesn't love you, he just thinks something *this* good should be shared around. Affairs are his *liaison d'etre*: I cheat, therefore I am. And at least he doesn't brag about his conquests — frankly, he doesn't have the time.

The Mad Rooter may be worth a one night stand (2000 Australian women can't be wrong) but marriage *would* be a mistake. Many think they can tame him but they usually change their minds at the altar, just after they've caught him goosing the matron of honour.

What motivates the Mad Rooter? Is it insecurity? Is it a secret fear that he is unloved? Is it a deep-seated yearning for human nurturing? No. He's just a randy dickhead with a hormone imbalance.

• MAN: THE MENU •

The Focaccia Kid

Aidan is arty, he's stylish, he's intellectual and this week he's taking you to a Ukrainian Film Festival. All thirty-seven excruciating hours of it. But at least it's better than last week, watching a volatile performance artist from Bogotar splatter the audience with pig bladders. In a moment of candour Aidan admits he dropped his last girlfriend when, in a moment of honesty, she called Werner Herzog 'an up-himself wanker'.

Aidan exists on a strict diet of focaccia, Camel cigarettes, short black coffees and sun-dried anythings. Chances are he'd eat your old gym boots if they were sun-dried and served up in extra virgin olive oil.

Beneath the surface you can see that Aidan is just an insecure soul trying desperately to reinvent himself. But that doesn't mean you've got to put up with him once he starts goose-stepping through your flat in his Doc Martens, sneering at your lifestyle and deriding your floral doona cover.

You've got to give this guy the flick and luckily there's one sure-fire way. You draw him aside and whisper the unforgivable: 'Darling, Diane was right — Werner Herzog *is* an up-himself wanker. And so, for that matter, is Wim Wenders.'

And so it's ciao, Aidan. Phew! Time to get a nice cup of Bushells and catch up with the plotlines in *Melrose Place*.

The Bloke's Bloke

He's a star graduate of Blokes' School, a Man's Man, a Bloke's Bloke, a Dickhead's Dickhead. And proud of it. He's a shorts and thongs man; the sort of fella who breaks things just so he can fix them, and enjoy the resulting testosterone rush. The Bloke's Bloke comes complete with a shed. His may be on the small side — but, as he points out, it's extendable.

There are plenty of things worse than ending up with a Bloke's Bloke. For one thing, he's mystified as to why other men have affairs. Don't they have any downpipes to plug? Don't they have any footings to jack up? The Bloke's Bloke is as loyal as a dog and he'll defend you to the death. It just would have been nice to know what he was thinking these past five years. But a Bloke's Bloke keeps the traditional bargain: woman talk, while men stare off into the middle distance.

The Tailgater

Jay talks fast, drives fast and mainlines books on positive thinking. He's so frantic his electronic organiser has just charged him with harassment. And so stressed out that his drink of choice is Mylanta.

Jay rollerblades while he talks on his mobile phone. He listens to motivational tapes in the shower. And somehow he just can't get relaxed under a palm tree; this guy can only relax when under a general anaesthetic.

We've all seen men like Jay. He's that motor mouth in the red sports coupe who's flashing his lights as he tailgates you. Let's face it, he has three erogenous zones: his ego, his penis and his car. And lucky you — you're allowed to stroke all of them. Except, of course, the car.

The Man Who's Let Himself Go

Five years ago he was a rangy, good-looking spunk, with every woman in town trying to get into his pants; these days, he can barely fit into them himself. He's let himself go. It took five years for him to go from a washboard stomach to an endearing little tummy. And another nine months for that tummy to go full term. Suddenly the truth hits you: your bloke's stomach is growing on an exponential curve. At this rate, by the end of the decade he'll be ordering a pair of Levi's 501s, and he'll be talking size.

He's still fun and easy to be around, but perhaps the problem is that he doesn't get enough exercise. Certainly you're growing quite concerned: if he doesn't move off that couch soon, the authorities may get suspicious and demand an autopsy.

Techno-man

Techno-man has spent his early life communicating through a keyboard — but now, with a shy stammer, he's asking you to interface. You'll just have to help him out: this may be the first time he's tried to access something without using a manual.

Techno-man is gentle, he's smart, he's introverted — and up to now the only thing that's ever gone down on him is his computer. Late at night you'll find him, on line to cyberspace, and that's when you'll have to drag him away from the terminal — and demand that he logs on to you.

This man will never call up other women, just other programs. And sure, those computer programs can beat you hands down in differential calculus, but can they cut it in a silk chemise?

One of the Boysies

When he is on his own, your colleague is a sensitive, intelligent, mature citizen of the nineties. But then he bumps into a few of his mates around the photocopier — and an unscheduled meeting of The Boys' Club is suddenly in session. Before your eyes this competent 38 year old man regresses to a naughty fifteen-year-old schoolboy, snickering with his mates.

You can't exactly hear their conversation, but a few key words float across the office. 'Fwooar.' 'Hugies.' 'Norks.' Benny Hill might be dead, but his spirit lives on.

From the constant nervous glances over their shoulders, they know they are doing wrong; these men are walking wild, living dangerously on the wrong side of the law. If their partners ever get to hear of this, they'll be dead meat.

What strange herd instinct drives these men? Once around the metaphorical keg it seems some primitive synapse connects, and all they are capable of is suggestive remarks and some heavy-duty ogling. Yes, that's right — it's not so much that they are playing the Fool; more that they've all become King Leers.

And after ten minutes you've had enough ... so you shoulder your way through to the photocopier. Horrified, they realise there is a non-bloke in earshot, and like frightened rabbits they scatter back to their desks — six aging schoolboys, caught in the act.

Recess is over, and you've just rung the bell.

CHAPTER TWELVE

THE BATTLE OF THE SEXES

A Final Word

"By the fifteenth century the age of individualism had arrived, meaning that men got to be individuals while women got to do the washing-up. This struck men as such a marvellous idea that it was left in place for the next four hundred years."

The war of the sexes appears to date from the earliest stages of evolution — when the first sexually differentiated amoebas noticed the male amoebas were getting the lion's share of the zooplankton. But with the arrival of humans, the situation worsened. Cro-Magnon man, for instance, finally learned to stand upright, but only because Mrs Cro-Magnon was trying to vacuum beneath his feet.

Always there was the tension. Indeed, Stone Age drawings have recently been found showing cavemen wearing washing-up gloves — the first documented case of tribal women participating in what is known as 'the dreaming'.

By the Middle Ages men were already avoiding their domestic responsibilities by staying late at work. In the cases of some military men this extended to thirty years at the Crusades — with the men promising that, just as soon as they got home, they'd spend some 'real quality time' playing hopscotch with their 48-year-old-twins.

By the fifteenth century the age of individualism had arrived, meaning that men got to be individuals while women got to do the washing-up. This struck men as such a marvellous idea that it was left in place for the next four hundred years.

But the Renaissance offered woman new opportunities to dabble in all manner of activities. Not only could a woman wash up, she could also cart water, chop wood and scrub the mould off the moat. And all while she was eight months pregnant with number thirteen.

Yes, she was free as a bird to create any work of genius she wanted — and to sign it with the traditional nom-de-plume of the woman artist, *Anon*. Nevertheless, generations of Anons proved dangerously imaginative, forcing man to slow down her success by inventing the corset for the seventeen-inch waist. Later still, further obstacles were developed, including the step-in, the high heel, the stiletto, platform shoes and, perhaps most excruciating of all, bikini wax.

But as each generation of woman has overcome these handicaps, man has had to invent new ones — thus providing an important engine for human progress. It is a little known fact that the moon landing was merely an elaborate scam to get Neil Armstrong out of having to take the children to the holiday matinee of *Chitty Chitty Bang Bang*.

Yet still women searching for equality moved forward. Or, in the case of those still wearing platform shoes, stumbled forward, twisting their ankles and ending up face forward in the mud.

Thank goodness that in these days of the post-industrial era everything's different. Today, men continue to contribute to our society, but now that contribution is matched by that made by women. Just as soon as they've finished the washing-up.

Mapping the Modern Man

Why have men, throughout history, been so full of themselves? The truth is that blokes do some things really, really well. For a start, they can reverse park under pressure — and do so while making an obscene hand gesture to the bloke they've just beaten to the spot. They can also get a bad haircut, and blame the barber and not themselves. They can order their own dessert, and to hell with the kilojoules. And they can look in the mirror in the morning, and no matter how daunting the reflection they can still mumble to themselves, 'Mmm, not bad.'

These are all things that women could learn from men. After all, wouldn't it be better if women liked themselves as much as men like themselves? Or is there not room in the world for *that* much self-love?

Yes, men love themselves — but women love them too. Whatever

• THE BATTLE OF THE SEXES •

THE Y-CHROMOSOME OR WHY, OH WHY, ARE MEN LIKE THEY ARE?

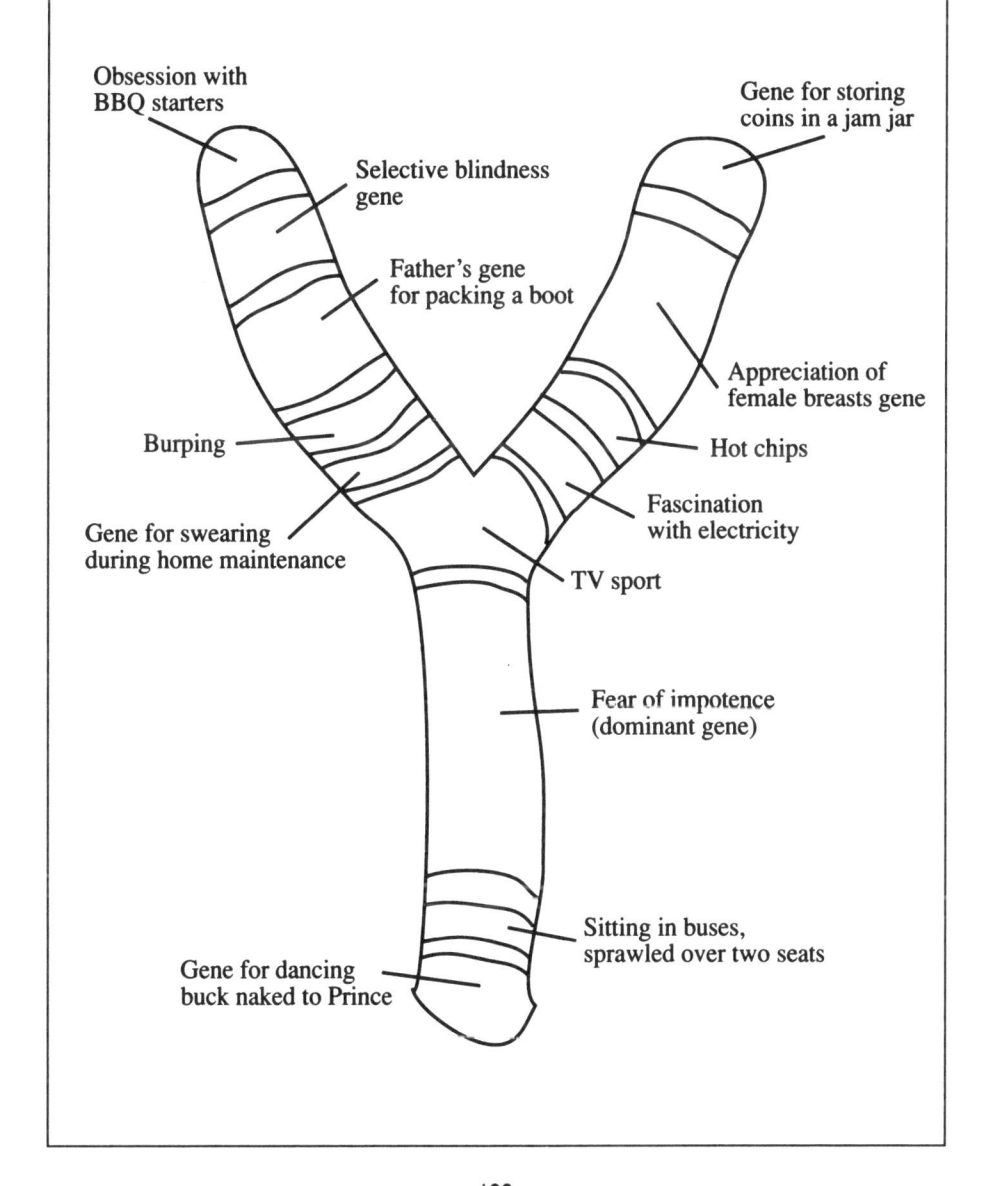

- Obsession with BBQ starters
- Selective blindness gene
- Father's gene for packing a boot
- Burping
- Gene for swearing during home maintenance
- Gene for storing coins in a jam jar
- Appreciation of female breasts gene
- Hot chips
- Fascination with electricity
- TV sport
- Fear of impotence (dominant gene)
- Sitting in buses, sprawled over two seats
- Gene for dancing buck naked to Prince

the drawbacks of living with a man, they have many virtues. They look great in a dinner suit. They can reach very high up. They may own a socket set.

And just sometimes, when a certain man comes out wet from the shower, all shiny and clean, with his torso swaying above the knotted towel, you may even go so far as to use the word 'adorable'.

We live in a time of change, when gender roles are being constantly challenged. And men need to know what women *really* want. Do they want a tough man or a sensitive man; a talker or the strong silent type; a decision maker or a negotiator.

And most important of all, if women are going to take so long making up their minds, could the blokes just slip out for a few cleansing ales in the meantime?

All the rules have changed. Should he open the car door? Who should pay for dinner? And how should he treat his female boss? It's now considered impolite, for instance, to give up your seat to a woman (unless it's on the Sydney Stock Exchange).

For blokes it's very confusing. Women criticise men all the time, and say they have to change — but why should they? The men are the ones wolfing down chocolate mudcake and hollering out to their brother-in-law to crack open the second slab. Aussie men may have endured thirty-five years of stern feminist criticism for their empty values, but they'll be buggered if they feel *that* empty, especially after the third slice of mudcake.

• THE BATTLE OF THE SEXES •

The Wide, Wide, Wide, Wide World of Blokes

The world is full of drop-dead gorgeous women who are convinced they are ugly and of men who — for no good reason — believe they are Rampant Sex Gods. The women may be virtually perfect, but they will fixate on their one imperfection, however tiny. And so there will be this absolute goddess walking down the beach, and she will be totally convinced that everyone is glaring at her fat ankles.

Meanwhile Michelin Man is rolling into view: 163 kilos of muscle, fat and inflated self-regard. The tummy's no longer taut, the shoulders are lumpy, the buttocks have long lost their fight with gravity. And he, too, is preoccupied with thoughts about his physical appearance. 'I bet everyone's thinking,' he mumbles to himself, 'about what a top bloke I am.'

Or at least that's what he's mumbling about until the second he sees the gorgeous woman walking towards him, her glistening cossie defining the slow roll of her hips, and her perfect breasts lilting as she moves. And at that moment, of course, all thoughts about himself disappear. 'Cor,' he thinks, '*she's* got fat ankles.'

What a shame he can't do a direct comparison with his own ankles. Mainly because he hasn't seen them since 1981.

The Bald Facts

At the end of the day it's all a question of propaganda. Take a male problem like balding. Who but a man could dream up the unlikely sales pitch that 'bald men are more virile'. It's like a woman with varicose veins going up to a man, winking naughtily and proclaiming: 'Get a look at these, honey — they're a sign of fertility.'

Yes, the male propaganda machine would leave Stalin speechless. Listen to blokes talk, and every man is a Girl Magnet. It's an ego-fest that extends from the armies of small men chanting 'small men, big libido' right through to the crowds of dyslexic men proclaiming 'dyslexic men, dig bicks'.

It's easy to laugh at men for their self-confidence, but it would be wrong for womenfolk to laugh *too* hard and long. After all, it will only deepen those unsightly wrinkles. Remember the social rules: when men get old and weather-beaten they get called 'distinguished'; when women get old and weather-beaten they get called 'old and weather-beaten'.

The result is of course that the male psyche is strong and resilient. Many Australian men have travelled thousands of kilometres through India and Tibet, studying the ancient arts of Buddhist meditation, in a noble attempt to dissolve their own ego. All a woman has to do, on the other hand, is spend a morning trying on jeans at Grace Brothers, with three mirrors, a fluorescent light and a pair of size 10 jeans.

Blokes and Self-Esteem

or Blokes who Love Themselves Too Much

Self-esteem, as we have noted above, is the central difference between the sexes. But at least Australian men are trying to help each other out. Aware that there's a problem, at least they are trying to chip away at each other's excess self-regard.

Why else would your bloke habitually greet his best buddy with the phrase 'G'day you ratfaced dickhead'? And why else would his buddy reply: 'I'm fine, you weak-as-piss bastard'?

Strange as it may seem, these are terms of endearment. They are the Aussie bloke's way of expressing the deep love that wells in his breast whenever he spots his mates.

'Loser', 'clueless joke', 'dork-featured rock-ape', 'chinless drongo', 'short-arsed deadhead', 'randy meat-head' — all these are signs your bloke is feeling some very special and tender emotions.

You may reckon that Aussie men have tickets on themselves. But this has been achieved despite receiving 200 years of horrendous verbal abuse — especially from their best friends. Imagine how insufferable they'd be if they started paying each other compliments.

Thus Mother Nature in her wisdom redresses the imbalances in a culture.

The Naked Truth

Yet still blokes feel amazingly positive about themselves — so positive that they like nothing better than wandering about the house buck naked.

Eating cornflakes? It's best done naked. Dancing to Lyle Lovett? Nude's the only way. Collecting the mail? Well, maybe *your* bloke's got a serious problem.

But around the house it *is* strangely common for men to wander naked and free — striding over the savannah that is your living room carpet. For most males life is just one long glorious streak. Why hide the goods under the counter, they ask, when they could be giving pleasure to others — right there in the shop window. After all, admiring their body gives *them* enormous pleasure, why not you?

Women may knock it, but they'd love to have this sort of confidence — a confidence that not only allows blokes to express themselves without a shred of clothing but also allows them to express an opinion without a shred of factual information.

Blokes are experts on everything. And if you think it's irritating when he tries to tell you how to do your job, just wait until you're giving birth and he kindly whispers, 'Darling, you're pushing all wrong.'

It's said that men have been trained by the patriarchy to block their feelings and become strong silent types, but today's new man seems able to express his feelings for hours at a stretch — most particularly on the topic of his sad inability to express his feelings.

But still there's a difference between men and women. Consider, for example, the sort of self-help books on the market for women and imagine them rewritten for Australian men. You can practically see them on the shelves:

The Male Mystique

I'm Drinking As Fast As I Can

Intelligent Men, Bimbo Brides

Men Who Love Themselves Too Much

and, of course, that male classic,

I'm OK, You're F——ed.

Treaty Time

Perhaps it is finally time for a treaty between the sexes — in which both sides would make some concessions. Men could agree not to sit on the bus with legs sprawled across two seats. And women could order their own desserts, instead of the current situation where they say 'Oh, no, nothing for me', and then snitch all their bloke's *crème brulee.*

The contested territory that is the bathroom could be handed over to the woman, just providing she promises not to use the 'female we' as in the phrase 'we painted the shed'. Especially when her bloke's got the blood blisters to prove he did it all.

And men could agree not to drink milk straight from the carton at night when they think no one is looking. Just as long as perfectly healthy and sexy women agree not to talk endlessly about their supposed weight problems.

And so on, and so on.

But meanwhile, somehow, the sexes manage to live together. And women still, at least occasionally, find the Aussie man irresistible.

How does one explain their eternal appeal? They may be playfully insulting their pals, admiring their good looks in the mirror, or stretching credulity about the positive side of baldness — but who cares? The heterosexual Australian woman has had generations of practice at recognising the best side of that guy under the car — even when he's out there buck naked changing the sump oil and hollering for another slice of mudcake.

He may not be the man you married, but at bedtime, when the late-night tennis is in recess and the washing-up is done, the romance can still flicker into passion. And you may find that, even within the heart on an Aussie bloke, there are things tender and sweet to be found.

That's the point. Blokes will always be a problem with which women need to wrestle. But preferably in front of a roaring log fire.

INDEX

Adair, Red 47
Air Guitar 84
auto-eroticism 13
BBQ starters (fiddling with) 9
Big Bird, ménage à trois with 71
Blind Freddie 26
Blokes' School 28
Bobo the cat, composting of 82
bra catalogue 98
Brunswick Green 83
bum, splinter in 72
Carry On Nurse (bosoms of) 107
child-eaters 73
chilli monkey brains 102
chinless drongo 137
Chitty Chitty Bang Bang 132
commercial break (sex during) 59
Count von Luckner's yacht 17
Deadly Beijing Mongrel Killer Flu 107
deck-size, comparison of 103
dog curry 102
dork-featured rock-ape 137
F-Wit's Flood Buster 10
Fwooar (female) 61
Girl Magnet 136
glow-in-the-dark butterfly cards 71
Herzog, Werner 125
Hill, Benny 128
Hills Extendaline 77
Howard, John 95
hugies 128
Intelligent Men, Bimbo Brides 138
Judaeo-Christian culture 44
Kama Sutra for Parents 70
King Leer 128
Leach, Thomas, birthday party of 27
leeches, live 106

leisure wear 91
Lysistrata 51
Macpherson, Elle (appreciation of) 41
mad rooter 124
Mambo surgical truss (100%) 82
Mickey On Ice 82
money, shitloads of 85
Mr Dropsie 64
Mrs Cro-Magnon 131
Ms Stetson's maths class 58
musk ox, wrestling of 14
Ning, Nang, Nong, in the 72
norks 128
Nostradamus 123
Pajero, its role in mid-life crisis 81
rampant sex god 135
rash (used as ice-breaker) 23
Richards, Keith (liver of) 84
Rio underpants 92
Rural Lands Protection Board 85
Sanjay's Hot Indian Curry House 102
Smithfield Truck Parts 7
spongy-bottoms (in men) 101
Stone, Sharon 60
Stunt Housework 47
Sydney Stock Exchange 134
Tantric Sex 69
Taxation, Deputy Commissioner of 60
vibrating bed 44
waaaahhhhh 74
wheely bin, sex in 60
white pointers 63
Wolfe, Naomi 123
Xerpotz 72
Yucky Bits 29
Zappa, Frank (the late) 83